Life on the Pipe

Life on the Pipe

Charles Calvin Barber

To order additional copies of this book, contact:
Xlibris Corporation
1-888-795-4274
www.Xlibris.com
Orders@Xlibris.com
90294

CONTENTS

I would like to dedicate this Book to My lovely Auntie, Ms. Jacqueline A. Jackson and My Beautiful Daughter kewon Sims. Most of all, I like to thank God for the Strength to Write this Book! Last but Not lease, thank Ms. Carol Washington for helping Me with this Book!

Drawing of Mother Katrina Depicting her faith during Hurricane Katrina.

CHAPTER 1

MONEY & POWER & DRUGS

At the Age of 20, I WAS on top of the World with 48,000 Dollars I could call my own. My Possessions was a 1984 Honda magna Motorcycle, a Shotgun liquor house, and well furnished Apartment. I Mean, I had women from an Age Range of 16 to 44. But Most of all, I was dealing Reefer for a Professional Wrestler which I Choose to Keep his name confidential I can Honestly Say that 1984 was the best Years of My life. I was Receiving .2 lbs. every week from my Connection for $650.00 Each. I Actually Made $1300.00 off Each pound of reefer I would Splurge money, and weed on Big Parties & lots of expensive Clothes & jewelry. I was a Single Man and Choose to live the Single life with one of my Older Brothers. We Shared Our Money Growth with Serious intentions of Having the best Damn liquor house in Salisbury N.C. I took Pride in my Bootleg liquor house. My Liquor house became so popular & well known for the Cleanliness and the luxury of the furniture and Hospitality. People came from Charlotte to Greensboro to buy the Grade A Reefer we Sold.

Money was Pouring in so Fast we could barely Spend it. We served top name Beers & Liquors for the Customers. We Even delivered drinks to the neighbors & Kept the near by neighbors lawns cut to keep them from Complaining to the Police. We stayed on our P's and Q's To keep any Commotions down.

I Remember Closing my liquor house late one night. I Put Everyone out about 1:30 AM. I wanted to count my money Stash, a week had passed Since I last Checked it. I kept all the money from Reefer Sells under My

Bed Mattress, and The liquor & Beer Money in the Kitchen Cabinet. My Biggest Concern was the Money Under the Mattress. I Raised the Right Side of the Mattress and I was stunned to see how Much Money there was. I counted & Recounted. I kept Coming up with $48,000. My Heart Skipped a Beat. I couldn't believe this was Actually My Money, not Counting the Money that was building Up in the Kitchen Cabinet. I Counted at least $ 700.00 In 5's, 10's & 1's. My heart Thumped like a fast beating Drum, I stopped all Movement To Stare at the front & BACK doors of the Shotgun house.

For the Very first time in my life I was Scared Shitless. I needed real protection not the Protection that your Mother and Father gives you. But the Protection of Blue-Steel. I need a gun, I said to myself Under my Breath. My Hands are well trained in Hand to Hand Combat, But These Hands ain't Worth jack-Shit to a Pistol. So I Manage to Calm Myself down and fell asleep at the Kitchen table Close to the Butcher Knife.

The Very next Morning I Arose from the Kitchen table With the same Clothes on my back to PURCHASE A 38 Special from the Black-Market.

The 38 Special Came with a Box of 50 Bullet Shells. I remember giving the guy $75.00 and A Ounce of Reefer for the Total PACKAGE. After leaving his Car I quickly Stuffed the 38 Special in the front of my Pants and the Bullets in my BACK Pocket.

As I walked on the BACK Streets of Salisbury, I felt a sense of Pride, and Boldness. I Reached down in the front of my Pants Very gently to Examine The Hot Pistol. Now I wanted to put this Baby to the test. I Got 6 Shells from the box of Bullets and Carefully Placed them in the 38 Special. I Closed the Chamber, held it over my head, and let off all Six Rounds Quickly.

I Could feel the Rush flowing through my nervous Body. I WAS feeling Powerful & UNTOUCHABLE. I Quickly Stuck the gun BACK into My Pants as I Continued to walk the back Streets. Suddenly I felt a SURGE of Heat BURNING Close to my nuts. I forgot that the Gun Was heated from the gun powder. So I Quickly Reached down in my Pants, Snatched the gun out, And threw it on the ground. That taught me a Valuable lesson after Shooting a loaded gun.

After making my transactions with My Close friend, I MANAGE to WORK My Way BACK home, only to See the front Screen Ripped off the Edge of the Window. My plants and flowers were Knocked Over as if someone broke into my Liquor house. So I grabbed my gun, loaded It outside, and Opened the front door. The liquor house was neatly intact Except for the front Window, and the BACK Window. Someone had Climbed in the front window, Stole the Remaining REEFER out of My Kitchen Cabinet along with the $700.00 in Small Bills & Change, and Helped themselves out of the BACK Window.

I Unlocked the BACK door to See if I could find Some type of Evidence. The only Clue I Came up With was, whoever broke into my house WORE A Size 8½ Dingo Boot. So I Rush BACK into the house to See what else was missing. I PRAYED as I lifted Up the Bedroom mattress. A sigh of Relief came over Me when I Saw the 48 gs Still there. But the Anger WAS still there also. I started my way out the BACK Door with the 38, still in my hands with finger on the trigger, Ready to Blow Whoever this Bitch-Ass-nigga Away. The Boot prints led to a PASS through the BACK YARD leading towards the BACK Streets of Salisbury. I Closed My Liquor House for that Day only to investigate on who broke into My House. I Thought to Myself, "Who comes to My Liquor House that wear Cowboy boots?" Then it Struck me that the Only person WEARING Cowboy Boots is My half-Brother, Ronnie-Joe. Everything was coming BACK to Me. I Remember him the night before asking for Credit, But I Made it My business not to give credit to the Unemployed. The night was Creeping' Up on me, so I had to make a move Quick before Ronnie-Joe Spent the Money & Reefer running the Street life. I had to think like he would think. I kept Saying' to myself, "Where Could he be"! Where would he go on a Saturday Nite. Surely he wouldn't be dumb Enough to Spend the money, and Sell the Reefer in town. I thought to myself, He's going out of town to Party hard in Lexington. N.C. To the Club called the "bow-Knots", The bow-knots is WELL Known For staying' open untill the EARLY MORNING light. So I Manage to get on my motorcycle, and Cruise to the night Club. When I Pulled up, the Bow-Knots WAS in FULL-Swing. The PARKING lot was PACKED with Young & Old males and females. I Mean, there was all types of Beautiful tenderoni's there. Even the store Across the Street was full of laughter and Beer drinking' & Reefer Smoking. I Really Enjoyed this type of Atmosphere. All The Dogs looking for some Satisfaction from female Dogs. But Pussy was the LAST thing on my Mind. Finding Ronnie-Joe was the first thing on my mind, So I PARKED my Motorcycle at the Store Parking lot between Two nice Motorcycles to conceal my Presence.

I Avoided Any type of Conversation with the Two Beautiful Females walking Across the parking lot. So I Quickly crossed the Busy Streets of the night, and Faded in with the Outside crowd of People in the Bow-Knots PARKING LOT.

I Could feel the Presence of DANGER in the warm night air. My instincts were telling me that Ronnie-Joe was in Close distance. I knew from the PAST that Ronnie-Joe was no Easy Victory in hand to hand Combat. His Reputation for fighting' made him stand out in the crowds. I Remember a few years BACK in his high-school days, He was the all-state Conference Champion Wrestler in his division. His nick name in High School was the "Wildcat". He was known for his hand Speed, and Masculine Strength on the Wrestling mats. He weighed about 220 lbs., with Muscles in his arms & legs as if Someone carved him out of Stone.

His stature was about 5' 8" with DARK green cat like Eyes. I Feared this man in my YESTER-years, Cause I was Considered a Youth in His High-School DAYS. But Years have PASSED and I Too have gained a Powerful Reputation of being devastating with Awesome hand Speed. I also earned a nick-name "THE HIT-Man". My friends gave me the nick name because my Boxing Style was compared to the professional boxer, Thomas HERNS A.K.A. THE HITMAN:

My thoughts were interrupted by Another Brother of Mine. He was in the Club Parking lot Rapping to three beautiful black females who just came out the Bow-Knots for some night air. I Manage to ease my way towards My brother Reggie. Silence fell on their lips as I Approached the three Beautiful ladies, and My Brother Reggie. They Knew from the Expression on my face that something was troubling Me. My eyes held the look of hatred. The Butt of My 38 Special Stood out between my Shirt & Pants. I wanted my gun to be seen by the Beautiful ladies. I Could see them out of the corner of my eye as I walked up on My Brother Reggie. "WHERE'S Ronnie Joe" I stated in a low Tone of a whisper. I followed his Eyes moving towards the side of the Night Club. The first thing to catch my Eyes was the Dingo Boots he was wearing on his feet. I Saw Ronnie Joe making A transaction. He was Actually Hustling Reefer. My damn Reefer that was stolen out My House. He never saw me as I walked up on him. He had his back turned still Making his transaction. When I tapped him lightly on his Right Shoulder I held my fist in a Squeezing' position. (Firm & Tight). He never had a Chance to see what knocked him out or who hit him, I caught him Straight between his Eyes with my fist. He dropped to the ground AS if Someone let the air out of a balloon. He fell in a mud puddle face first, The Crowd fell Silent as I began to Stomp his face deeper & deeper in the Mud. At the Same time I was Yelling and Screaming, "You Rotten motherfucka the next time you break into my house, I'll bust a CAP in Your ass, You punk Motherfucka GET UP, GET UP! My intentions were to Shoot him in the leg so he won't come looking for me the next day. But I really didn't see any need too. He was hurt bad! "All EYES were on me" As I walked back Across the Street to the store. I was so damn Hyped from Knocking out the Wildcat. I Completely forgot about getting the Money & Reefer he Stole from me.

I WAS more concerned about the fame and Respect Everyone would give me after beating the Shit out of a stone cold brawler. Months passed by after that.

Things were going Smooth Again in Salisbury N.C. My fighting Reputation was known throughout the Town, and "So was My liquor house". I had more friends than I ever wanted. I WAS Introduced to this black guy By the name of "RAZOR", we became the best of friends He Spent Over 200.00 a day 'buying' Reefer. He spent so much money buying' weed, I'd give him beer & liquor on the house. I treated him Very Special. He also Knew Plenty of White folks which brought more business to the liquor house. My liquor-house became so popular I gave the house a name "THE RAZZLE DAZZLE" It was Everything in one! A LIQUOR HOUSE, GAMBLIN' HOUSE, FREAK SHOW HOUSE, REEFER HOUSE, Etc, I Had so much Fun in the RAZZLE DAZZLE I gave up the apartment I Rented Next door. I Couldn't Afford another break in. So I moved The furniture I had in my apartment to My stepfather's House to Stay in the liquor house A.K.A. RAZZLE DAZZLE.

I Even let the RAZOR Spend A Couple nights with me. He was homeless, but I had A Heart for him.

One Morning we drove out for breakfast at the waffle House when He made a Statement saying . . .

"Peanut," You can make a damn Killing Selling Cocaine. I knew nothing About Selling Cocaine, Only Reefer!

I Asked, How much Money are you talking about? HE Said, Peanut, Do you have $300.00. Yeah Why! I Replied He told me I Can triple the sales of Reefer if I invest in buying an eight-ball, So I Kept Silent Until We drove back to the RAZZLE DAZZLE. I told him to Stay out-Side a few Minutes. I locked the Door Behind Myself and Quickly I walked to the right Side of My Bed to lift the mattress. I grabbed 3 One hundred dollar bills and gave Razor the Money. "He WAS Shocked" I Replied "Go ahead" Do WHAT You gotta Do. I even let him Use my Motorcycle to go make the transactions. He made a Phone Call, hung up the Phone, Picked up the Motorcycle Keys, and told me, His Connection wanted to meet him in the parking lot of K-MART In 30 minutes. He was excited to Make the transaction. I didn't Know if he was excited to ride on my new motorcycle, or to get Some Cocaine.

Well, Everything went Smooth between the two Making the transaction, He was back at the RAZZLE DAZZLE Within 35 minutes and I was pleased to See RAZOR make it back in One Piece. I WAS worried About My damn bike More than Him getting the dope.

I Could See the excitement on Razor's face when He hopped off the Bike. He Was Yelling my name from Outside . . . NUTCRACKER! NUTCRACKER, I made the Connect NUTCRACKER! "Open the door NUTCRACKER" Hell, I Even got Excited to let him in to See What he Purchased. LET ME SEE WHAT You GOT RAZOR, DAMN!

He Pulled out Piece of White Powder in a plastic bag about the Size of a Ping Pong ball. I Said, with Anger in my Voice, "Boy" you Paid $300.00 dollars of My Money for this little Bit of Shit"! He Said, NUTCRACKER, We can make damn near 700.00 dollars off this little Bit of Shit. I Couldn't Control My Anger, SPARKS Shot from my eyes at him. I Could See fear in his Eyes. He said, Peanut! trust Me. get a mirror, and a few Sandwich Baggies. "TRUST Me"!!! My Body Stood Motionless for about 3 minutes. The only thing I Could think about was busting a CAP in his ass. So I decided to give him a Chance, I Snapped back to my Senses, Snatched the Mirror off the Wall in the bedroom, Rushed to the Kitchen cabinet to get a box of sandwich bags With a razor blade. I Watched RAZOR with death eyes, praying' that He Come Correct With the Money he Promised. I observed him Carefully as he Cut the Corner of the baggies With the razor blade. His hands moved Swift,& Quick with the Corner of the blade. I Sit In my favorite chair thinking to Myself, Wondering how did he get the nick-name RAZOR. from looking at him Slicing the baggies with Speed & Perfection, He had to have gotten the nick-name for being an expert with a blade. Before my mind Drifted any further, he was finished bagging up the dope.

Each bag was wrapped individually. I Counted 35 bags, the Size of A match head. He Said, NUTCRACKER This is $700.00 dollars worth, I Can Make You 600.00 If You give me 2 days to Sell it. I Told him with Anger in my Voice "RAZOR", I'm giving You 2 days Exactly To get my damn Cash, Cause if you don't, Don't worry about Staying in Salisbury no more, and that's my Word. I Demanded him to get the fuck out my face.

RAZOR left out my front door Saying . . . "TRUST ME, NUTCRACKER"

"COCAINE"

Two days later, the RAZZLE DAZZLE was in full Swing. With my Usual Customers, buying drinks, Playing cards, and Purchasing Dime Bags & Twenty bags. Suddenly, I heard the Voice of a name that only one person Called me by. "NUTCRACKER"! "NUTCRACKER"! "It's Me baby." It was the Voice of the Razor, calling my name from outside the Doorway. I stopped Serving drinks to my Customers to let RAZOR in the house. When I approached the front door, I Could hear laughter Coming from the Other Side of the door.

When I Open the door, 6 One Hundred dollar bills Flashed in my face. I Was Completely Shocked How quick Razor had flipped the little White bags. I noticed how sharply dressed RAZOR was from head to toe. I was

Speechless. After receiving $600.00 dollars before his deadline now I had Complete Confidence in RAZOR. "We" became the Best of friends.

I Accepted his friendship once again, We hung together like Peas & CARROTS, I Even bought an extra helmet for My Motorcycle just for him. RAZOR taught Me things I never Knew about Selling Cocaine We Started Putting' the White Powder in joints. RAZOR Would Call it frosted flakes. It made me feel Comfortably numb.

People called 'COCAINE, a Rich Man's High"! and I was Enjoying every minute of it "The Frosted Flakes", it was Something EVERYBODY was doing at the time. It took me to a different level! With almost 50,G's under my mattress and BUSINESS BOOMING left & right, I was feeling sensational.

I felt I was in the prime of my life At 20 years old, but Something WAS missing in my life. Even though I Thought I had it all! MONEY, POWER & RESPECT WAS MY DREAM, BUT something Was still Missing. I Went in Deep Meditation thinking of What was missing in my life . . . POW!!! IT HIT ME LIKE A TON OF BRICKS . . . "A Steady WOMAN".

Oh, don't get me wrong! I had women as far as the naked eyes Could See, But none to Call my Own, I Wanted A Woman that Would love me for ME not for What I have to give them, or the things I Could do for them. So the hunt was on . . . I Would travel Miles & Miles trying' to find My Soul Mate, But to No-Avail.

Then one After-noon When I had just come back from Picking up 2 lbs. of Reefer from my My Connection. I noticed two Beautiful females Sitting in a 1979 Chrysler Cordoba. As I pulled My Motorcycle in the yard, the two ladies got out of the Car. I Was familiar with the driver She Was dating My brother Anthony A.K.A, "FATCAT" I hired him to help me run the RAZZLE DAZZLE. Linda Was her name, but the pecan tan sister getting out on the passenger Side Made my heart Skip a beat. She was ABOUT 5'7 With a Coca-Cola Shaped body frame as if God took his own private time making her to perfection. Her eyes were hazel light brown like a black China Doll. Her teeth were pearly White as if the Sun Shined on them daily. This Woman Was neatly dressed, and Very Sophisticated looking with long beautiful jet black hair down to her Shoulders. I Wanted to make this Woman My lady!! And if She had any faults about herself, I

Damn-sho-Couldn't See them. "Cause In my Eyes, This was the one and only female for me."

As I got off my bike, Linda Said, "Hi peanut" I Want you to Meet a Close friend of Mine.

We looked Each Other Up & Down as if We were Sizing each Other up for a Boxing Match. I Greeted her With a Smile to Reveal My Pearly Whites. I noticed She Did the Same. We Couldn't take our eyes off One another. Linda broke the Silence by Saying, Peanut this is Leslie Leslie this is Peanut, I extended My hand to Shake her Soft hand Politely as possible. I broke the Silence, trying' to Sound as Sexy as Possible. "My My My" . . . So Your name is Leslie! I Replied. UUUM-HUUM, She Said In a tangible Voice. I've heard a lot about you Mr. Barber "Please" Leslie, Call Me by My nick-name . . . Peanut Will do okay baby. She Continued to Smile and Said okay peanut.

So what brings you two lovely Creatures down my way! I Stated in my Sexiest Voice. My brothers girl Linda broke in the Conversation to Say. I'm looking for "FAT CAT" to get me a nice dime bag. She extended a ten dollar bill to me as if I was FaT CAT.

"I Said, Fat cat isn't here right now, But I'm sure I Can manage to come up with a nice fat dime bag!"

I quickly told Linda to put her Money back in her Pocket, it's on Me! The Only Reason I Said that because I Wanted to Impress Leslie. I Invited them both in the Razzle dazzle for a drink of My finest alcohol "hennessy" Cognac.

Leslie was amazed by the layout My Liquor House. Her Eyes Scanned the Place as if She Was in La-La land. I eased over to the High Priced stereo to turn on Some Nice Rhythm & Blues on the radio. The Mellow Music filled living Room With a sense of Melody. I noticed Both ladies took their places in the Kitchen whispering to One another.

I Could See from the Corner of My eyes that both ladies were Checking me out. So I proceeded to remain Cool, Calm & Collective throughout the evening, during the time they were in the RAzzle Dazzle, not once did I Serve Leslie a drink of hennessy, nor did She Smoke Any of the Hog leg joints I Rolled for them. But my brothers girl Was trying to suck down everything in Sight. She Smoked Two Fat Ass Hog leg joints by herself, Plus damn near drank all my hennessy. But not once did her friend touch the Weed, or drink any booze, That made Me Show more interest in her.

I didn't want to make her feel out of Place, so I offered her Some orange Juice, or Soft drinks Since She wouldn't drink any alcoholic beverages.

She accepted My offer, So I gave her a glass of O.J. I Wanted to make this Beautiful black nubian queen My lady if it was the last thing I did.

hell, I tried to intoxicate the girl on orange Juice! It Seem like the More She drunk, and Spend time around Me. The More She Will conversate, and Open Up. To me, My Plan Was Working beautifully. I managed to get her full name address, and Phone number before they departed. My brother fat cat never Showed up for his Woman. I Kinda Hoped that he Would! That Would have given me Ample time to really get my mac on, Cause I was Destined To make Leslie

MY ONE AND ONLY QUEEN!!!

IT WAS DARK WHEN RAZOR Came To THE RAZZLE DAZZLE With another Eight ball of Cocaine. I WAS VERY hyper from meeting the Woman of My dreams. the only thing on my mind was Leslie. But the only thing on RAZORS Mind was the Cocaine. He helped himself to the Kitchen cabinet to get the plastic bags, and the Mirror off the Bedroom wall to cut the Dope Up.

Leslie's phone Number Was burning My Pocket up, But I didn't want to Seem too Anxious to make that Call. "Patience is a virtue" when trying' to get Someone you Want so desperately. RAZOR interrupted My thoughts by throwing A Frosted Flake joint on my lap.

"Fire it up NUTCRACKER"! HE said With Excitement. I Lit the Hog leg Frosted flake joint, took three Deep Puffs, and Past it back in his direction. He Completed bagging up the Cocaine and he was on a Mission Once Again. I Wasn't concerned about RAZOR blowing the Dope, or the Money. His Hustle game was Outstanding. He had my Complete trust Selling the Powder on the Streets of Salisbury. He Knew the Streets like the BACK of his hands. I Was Curious how he traveled When he Wasn't Using my motorcycle. One minute he was there, the next Minute he was gone. I really didn't care! as long as he came Correct with the Money. Once I gave him $300.00 dollars he would always come back 2 or 3 days later With $600.00 dollars, RAZOR WAS Running the Streets So much, he would Come to the house and Sleep for at least 10 or 12 hours. he was always welcome to rest his head at my Place.

One Morning he woke up in the Middle of the night Wanting to Use the Bike go to the waffle House. That's When I questioned RAZOR about transportation. He said that he had a 750 Harley Davidson Sportster. But it was in the Shop for Repairs. I Asked him How much would it cost to fix it. He Said, it was fixed and He Was Saving Money to get it out the Shop. I Asked him again, How much will it Cost to get the Motorcycle out. He said, $ 600.00 dollars, I Said, I'll take you to the Motorcycle Shop in the Morning to get it out for you. He Couldn't believe What he was hearing. So I gave him my word that I would pay for it, if he Wasn't lying about having a Motorcycle. RAZOR Was Wide Awake, now pacing the floor back & forth waiting on 9:00 o'clock to Come. Soon it Would be 9:00 o'clock, He Was Hype, and Ready to Ride to the Motorcycle repair Shop. I Pulled RAZOR about 7 Miles out of Salisbury To a Red-neck Motorcycle Shop. The Closer We got to the Shop, the More Excited RAZOR became. I noticed a Fat White-man With a long Red Beard hanging down to his Stomach Standing in front of a garage.

I stopped the Bike about 30 yards Before I got to him, to let RAZOR talk to him.

RAZOR, and The White Man Said a few Words and quickly disappeared into the Old beat Up garage. Within 5 Minutes RAZOR Came Running out of the garage, Yelling "NUTCRACKER" . . . give Me 600, It's ready!!! I Quickly gave him Six hundred dollars out of My Pocket. He Snatched the Money out of my hand and took off Running back in the dilapidated garage. Suddenly I heard a loud ROAR of a Motorcycle Engine. I Couldn't believe RAZOR was telling the truth. Before I Could get back on my bike, RAZOR Was Coming Around the garage on a 1979, Harley Davidson Motorcycle. It WAS BLACK, WITH CHROME WHEELS. I COULDN'T HELP MYSELF FOR LAUGHING AT THE TWO REBEL FLAGS HE HAD tied on the handle bars. He also had saddlebags on the Seat. I Thought to Myself . . . "A BLACK RED NECK!"

As We drove away from the Shop, We were Side by Side Riding down the Highway. I noticed he wanted to Blow The Motorcycle out Cause it was sitting in the garage for 4 months. I was probably paying for the Storage Fee, And the Motorcycle too, But just as long, as "RAZOR" Was happy, and as long as he didn't need to ask to ride my bike. IT WAS ALL GOOD! The roads were empty, RAZOR was ramming' His engine. I Knew exactly what he was getting at. HE wanted to race! THE race was on. But It didn't last long because I left Razor a quarter of a Mile in 3 rd gear.

Honda magnums are built for speed, I actually got high on Speed, Cause if i'm not pushing 140 mph. I'm not getting high!

Noon was approaching, We had been out riding all Morning. RAZOR & I Went our Separate ways on the Streets of Salisbury. He was like a Child With a new Toy on his Motorcycle, so I decided to Ride Solo to catch some peace of Mind.

And My Mind was on Leslie. I had her address & Phone number Memorized from looking at The napkin She gave me. Before I Knew it, I was at a Phone Booth dialing her number. The Phone rang twice before a Sweet Mellow Voice Said Hello. I replied Yes, May I Speak to Leslie. She replied this is she, who am I speaking to? "Peanut," I said in a low tone of voice. Do you have company? "No!" . . . not at this moment, Do you want me to have some company? She replied. No, not unless it's me I stated. "Peanut", I bet you can't even find your way to my house. Leslie, I bet you a steak dinner I can! "ALRIGHT," She replied. Within 20 Minutes. I was blowing the horn in front of an apartment complex. Her apartment no.# was 222. The Opening' of the door was Pleasant. A hand motioned FOR me to come in. I quickly got off my bike and Walked up the Side Walk that led to her apartment door, I was greeted with a Beautiful Smile from Leslie. I guess I owe you a steak dinner, huh?

Yeah! And I'd prefer if you cooked it here. She invited Me in her well furnished apartment. Everything was Well Kept and Neatly intact. Now I was in LA-LA land, Staring at Pictures on her walls, Hoping that She's living the Single life. My thoughts were interrupted by two little boys coming down Stairs. They Caught me by surprise, I wasn't aware that Leslie had Children.

Normally I hold Strikes against Women with Kids, But this was the Woman of my Dreams. If I wanted Leslie to be my QUEEN, I Had to Accept the total package. But I truly Wanted Leslie. I told myself, I won't look Any farther. As soon as the kids reached the bottom of the Stairs, I began to turn my interest towards them. This was the biggest front I'd Ever played. I wasn't concerned about them Damn Chaps. As a Matter of fact, The brats Would make things harder for me. Soon, I would learn to accept her Children. I Played my Cards to a tee after Putting over 72 hrs. in with the Kids, Leslie was all over me. She Said I showed her Kids too much Attention, and didn't Show her Enough. My Plan was working perfect.

The time came when Leslie asked me to spend The night with her. Those words were music to my ears, but I put on my best poker face, And told her I have a busy day tomorrow morning with FATCAT. She put

On her best puppy dog face with a frown to say, "please" . . . that was the magic word. I said, Leslie I'll Spend the night if you get me Up before 7:00 A.M.

Her eyes lit up lit up with sparks, she agreed to have me up before 7:00 A.M. I said to myself, "Peanut". Make this night last forever.

Within 30 minutes, Leslie had both Kids in bed asleep. I was in Leslie's bed Counting the remaining money in my wallet. I really enjoyed spending money on Leslie's two boys. Cause for one, I had it to Spend! I would buy Leslie groceries, pay her bills, Buy her boys bicycles and School Clothes etc.

I was learning to Accept the bitter with the Sweet. For the First time in my life, I found a good woman, that I Could express my inner most feelings too. She would Listen to my Boring Conversations, and Show Concern as if she was really interested in me. I guess that's why I loved her so much . . .

When Leslie entered the bedroom She was Wearing A long WHITE Nighty T-Shirt with a Pink teddy bear Painted on the front. Her hair was laid back on her Shoulders, as if she were a black goddess. I noticed the dark Pink finger-nail Polish on her one inch nails, not to mention her well Shaped legs. Leslie had the Body frame of A gymnast. I examined her from head to Toe, her skin Was Silky Smooth. She wore very little makeup, Leslie was the Perfect example of a natural beautiful BlACK QUEEN" Make-Up Would only enhance her beauty."

As I laid back on the bed with my head resting on two Pillows, I watched her hips Sway from Side to Side as she approached me. I could Smell the Sweet Perfume before She Entered the bedroom. I was wide Awake more than ever, as My nature grew. I wanted to take this beautiful woman and represent myself to her, but I Kept Saying to myself . . . "EASY PEANUT" you got all night. I Decided to foreplay with her Awhile. Leslie was 8 years older than me. I Said to myself, this is a lady, not a teenybopper! She was well experienced in having sex. Don't rush it Peanut!

As I Started Kissing Leslie on her Soft lips, We held our bodies Closer & Closer. My nature was at the peek of exploding. I Could hear her Soft moans. UUMMM . . . I Could feel her hips pressing against mine. The moans continued. OOOh! baby! I Wanted to take to her like a Wild Bull takes to his heifer. Suddenly, We heard crying from the next room. It was the crying of her youngest Son.

I Continued to lift her Nighty t-shirt up, but She Stopped Me, and Said. HOLD UP BABY . . .

Let me go Check on the Kids. I Slowly eased myself off her body, and laid on the left Side of the bed, as she walked into the next Room to Check on the kids.She Cut the Light on in the Children's Bedroom.

Now Both Boys were crying. I said To Myself, ain't this a bitch. I laid in the bed Waiting on her return. When she came back into the bedroom, She had both Kids in her arms trying to rock them to sleep. I Wanted to take the 2 DAMN BRATS, and lock there asses in the Closet. Leslie interrupted my thoughts by saying' . . .

Peanut . . . They're not used to Sleeping in the room by themselves. They usually Sleep with me.

Those words hurt! I Knew with both Kids Sleeping' in bed with Us, I didn't Stand as Chance getting the Pussy. I Could have choked the Shit out of them damn Kids. But As soon as both Kids, touched down in bed with us, they stopped crying . . . both kids were all over me, Sleeping So Peacefully. I Couldn't help but to love those boys! Within 45 minutes, We were all sleeping like One big family.

7:00 o'clock Came So quickly I Couldn't believe it, but there wasn't any need of Staying around. It was time for me to go back to WORK. Running the "RAZZLE DAZZLE" was my livelihood. If I Stayed here laid up with Leslie and the Kids, I Would Miss out on at least $800.00 dollars, So I Stayed around until Leslie fixed breakfast for me, and the Kids. After that She had to take the boys to PRE-School. Afterward She had to be to work at 8.00 am. Leslie was a very independent Woman; She was the mother & father to her Children. Later on, I questioned Leslie about her children's father, She Said he was in prison for Child support. I asked her did she Still love him. She stated, The love died years ago. after hearing those Words, I felt a sigh of Relief. At least I was in the front door. ON top of that! She Even had me a Key Made to Come over anytime I wanted.

The RAZZLE DAZZLE was 15 minutes away from Leslie's apartment. as I Got Closer to my house I Could See Some of My Usual liquor drinkers Waiting around to get their early Morning drink. Most of My Money was made from brick-YARD WORKERS & Textile Employees who worked

1st Shift. They were my best Customers, i trusted in giving out credit. They Always Paid their bills. After Serving about 7 OR 8 beer & liquor drinkers, i heard a loud roaring engine Coming down the street, The loud noise died in front of the house. I Knew exactly who it was . . . Razor! I Met him at the front door. I Could See the look on his face that Something WAS bothering him. I held the Door Open to bust a CAP in his ass. but I would have embarrassed us both by Shooting' in the neighbor-hood. He acted like he was scared to come inside So I broke the Silence by Saying . . . What the Fucks wrong! he Said, he fell asleep over a CRACK House, and got robbed, "I WAS furious"! I Went into the bedroom and grabbed My 38, Walked towards him Pointing the barrel at his Chest, Yelling angrily . . . "Where's My damn Money". His eyes got big as a boe dollar. I Repeated Myself Again . . . "Where's My Fucking Money"!!!

I Wanted to let him Know I was all about Business, so I fired off Three Shots Above his head.

He Squirmed liked a Pig getting Shot in the head. He Said, NUTCRACKER "NUTCCRAKER NUTCRACKER! Hold up NUTCRACKER, let me Explain! He was Checking himself to See if he was Shot. I Didn't Realize how Close I let off to his head. hell, it scared the Shit out of Me too. My intentions was to Scare razor just to See if he was lying. But he kept Saying the Same thing. He Repeated the Same Story about 12 times, and promise to pay me double.

That was the Very first time I disrespected My neighbors by shooting a gun in the neighborhood, every neighbor on the street Watched as I held a gun to a Man's head. I finally came to My Senses, and forced Razor into the house. He thought I was going to take him into the house to Bust a cap in his ass. But I embarrassed us both by Shooting' in the neighborhood.

I poured two drinks of Gin to Calm Our nerves. We both was Shaking like Cold Puppies. after drinking 3 More glasses of the Cheap Gin: Both of us WAS feeling Much better. Razor Explained that He was up for 3 days hustling, the next thing he knew, He was Asleep. He Said, When he woke up, Everyone in the house was High is a damn Kite. He look down at his pockets only to See Someone Cut Two Big holes on both Sides of his Pants. That was Kinda hard to believe Until I glanced Down at his jeans, Sure-nuff Razor didn't Even have Pockets. THAT WAS THE FUNNIEST!

Now here I am out of $600.00, And I'm laughing my ass off at Razor with no Pockets. I Decided to give Razor another Chance by giving him $300.00 TO GET STARTED.

So I made him Stand outside on the front porch because I didn't want him to See Where I was getting the Money from. I Quickly grabbed the Money and Put my gun back Under the Mattress.

Before I gave him the money, I warned him not to ever go to sleep in anymore CRACK-houses. I even gave him an Extra Hundred to buy himself Some more Pants, and for a Motel if he gets Sleepy. He drove his Motorcycle away from the Curve and down the road happy as a Hog Eating Slop.

It's 12:00 o'clock noon. The RAZZLE DAZZLE is in Full Swing With card gamblers & Liquor Buyers and Reefer Customers Coming and going.

My brother "FatCat" was in the back yard Cutting grass When I decided to Split our Savings. Before I came in to partnership with FatCat, I promised him that everything We Make, We'll Split straight down the Middle. So I decided to wait Until Every customer was out of the house Before we divided the Money.

It was about 3:30p.m. When the Coast was Clear. We locked the front and back doors. We Went in the bedroom to the Money Stash and Counted almost 50 G's. We both had $25,000.00 Apiece. Fat cat took his share of the Money, and Hid it In My Step fathers house. I decided to Keep My 25 G'S in the Same Place it grew from, under My bedroom mattress. We had so much Money to Call our Own, We would have two-day parties, rent NIGHT-CLUBS, go on SHOPPING' SPREES ETC, ETC." I started loaning Money out to family members. I Regret doing that because I never Saw that Money Again. They Say, Your family Members will Fuck you over quicker than Your So-called friends Will.

Well, Whoever Said that was So damn right. I tried to put a few of My brothers on their feet on giving them 1/4 lbs & ½ lbs, But no one never came back with the money! But What Could I do to them, they're my brothers. Oh, By the way! I have 10 brothers & 3 Sisters. I Love them all, but I love some more than others. WHY? We were raised in different households. They say I'm the craziest out of the bunch. I guess You will agree to that, after you finish reading' about "My Life on the Pipe".

After running the RAZZLE DAZZLE for almost 10 hrs. I decided to go Spend Sometime with Leslie and the Kids to get away from the Crowd. After receiving the Key to Leslie's apartment. I decided to surprise her by riding over without Calling. I parked My bike on the far Side of the Apartment Complex Walked Up to the front door and Stuck the Key in Without being noticed, or detected. I heard the television Up-Stairs in her bedroom, So I creeped upstairs with Caution hoping not to See Some no-name-Ass-nigga in the bed with her. But to My surprise
Leslie, and the boys were Sleeping peacefully by themselves. I Should have Known better than to to think She'd be foolish Enough to have Someone Over When she gave me the Key to her apartment.

As I Approached her Sleeping with both Kids Sound a Sleep in her arms. I Started caressing' her Silky Smooth Skin. I Bent over the bed and kissed her gently on those soft lips. She began to Open her Eyes to focus me in her sights! I quickly Put my index finger on her lips, and Whispered . . . "help me carry the Kids to their bedroom". I took my finger from her lips, and grabbed the Oldest boy while She held the younger Child in her arms. I led the Way to the next bedroom, Both Kids were Still in a deep Sleep. Leslie gently Pulled the Covers back From the children's bed. We Placed them Under the Covers and kissed them lightly on their foreheads. We tip toed back to the bedroom, and Shut the Door with ease. We looked at Each Other and smiled. I broke the Silence by Saying . . . So, let's Start Where We left off, My nubian queen. She put her arms around my neck, and kissed me on my lips. I Could feel the heat from her body. She was Sleeping in the Same Spot For hours, OR She was hot for me one. I held Leslie Close to Me Kissing her soft lips, Moving to her neck, Slowly Working my way to her breast. I Slowly backed Leslie to the foot of the bed. As she laid on her back with her arms extended out to me, I Slowly undressed myself, Starting with my Shirt then my Jeans, working my way down to my Boxers. Within 30 Seconds, I was naked as a JAY-bird Standing Over her. Her legs Spread Wider & Wider When she Stared at my oversized penis, I Knew For my age I was overly mature in Size.

I felt Everything would Equal up Just right, Cause Leslie was 28 with two Kids, and I WAS 20 Years of Age. So Leslie raised her legs, Motioning me to take her Panties off her gorgeous hips & well Shaped thighs.

I Took my time easing the Red Silk panties off Leslie as I Worked her panties below her Knees. My Eyes Focused on the Silky looking hairs on her Cunt. I was already hard as a Brick from Kissing & being caressed by her. But Now I Was hard as a granite Rock. She Managed to take the nighty Shirt off by herself. Leslie was staring up at Me with those hazel Eyes Putting Me in a trance, She broke the Silence Saying . . .

Do you Like WHAT YOU SEE BABY? I WAS SPEECHLESS WHEN I HEARD THE WAY SHE SAID THAT. MY lips Moved But My Body Moved faster. I WAS KNEELING OVER HER in a PUSH-UP Position. WHEN HER HANDS GRABBED MY hard Penis, She Rubbed it up & down on her Soft Silky Pubic hairs to insert Myself inside her body.

Her hips pumped up & down Slowly, our bodies Were moving to the Same Pace. I looked in Leslie's eyes, I Could See Pain written all over her perspiring face.

Her Voice trembled With Soft moans As Excitement began to build between the both of us. Our Kisses were passionate, our hearts were beating as one as I Exploded inside her world of Ecstasy. We Held Each others bodies Close to one another all Night, only to Fall asleep during the break of dawn.

Soon I was awakened by Leslie's two little boys as my Eyes began to Focus on the brats Jumping' up & down on the bed. I Could Smell the bacon Leslie was Cooking For breakfast downstairs. Suddenly a Sweet Voice from downstairs yelled to the Kids . . . Boys," Come and Eat!

As I laid back with both hands Resting on the back of My head, The Boys leaped From the bed & Raced Downstairs For breakfast. I Continued to think back on the passionate love making we Encountered only hours Ago. Patience was a Virtue, and It Was well Worth the Wait. I Put in almost a Month trying to get Leslie to be my main lady. Flashing my money, and Wining & Dining her was only, the beginning.

I had to be approved by Leslie's Mother. One day When I was over Leslie's apartment, her Mother Came Over to Check up on the Kids. Leslie & I were hugged up on the Couch When She helped herself in the Front door with her own Key.

I noticed how Leslie Eased Away from my Embrace and Squirmed herself to the Other Side of the Couch. Leslie's whole Attitude Changed when her mother Came over. I Continued to Sit on the Couch and watch Television. Leslie's Mother Called her into the Kitchen. She was CURSING, and RAISING hell about having a Stranger around her grandchildren, but little did She Know," I Was doing more For those Kids than her Fat Ass Ever did For them." Leslie's Mother practically Ran her life. But She wasn't about to Run My life. She Tried to Come between Leslie & I By threatening to have her Kids taken away if I continued coming around her. To this Very day, I never saw Leslie again cause her Mother made her Move out of town. I was Completely heart broken. The Lady of my life had abandoned Me, with the help of her hateful ass Mom. even today As I write this book I Want to Wish Leslie and her two boys' (Charlie & Tony) the very best in life.

At THE AGE OF 21, Things were going downhill for Me. My Cocaine habit was getting Worse & Worse, Depression had Set in on Me. I WAS blowing Money left & Right trying' to Find something to ease the Pain, BUT, TO NO AVAIL," I WAS BLOWING THOUSANDS & THOUSANDS OF DOLLARS ON FREE BASING COCAINE. I HAD taught MYSELF HOW TO COOK UP POWDER COCAINE FROM WATCHING experienced users. It seemed LIKE THE WHOLE TOWN WAS SMOKING COCAINE, EVEN THE FIRST LOVE OF MY LIFE HAD STARTED SMOKING ROCKS. THE FIRST LOVE OF MY LIFE WAS MY FATHER'S SISTER (JACKIE.) I MOVED OUT OF HER HOUSE WHEN I WAS 18 YEARS OLD, TO HAVE AN APARTMENT OF MY OWN IN SALISBURY. Smoking Reefer was common growing up, But I WAS curious How SMOKING COCAINE MADE ONE FEEL, So I Would Buy BIG Quantities of the White Powder from a guy who was Commuting Back & Forth from FLORIDA. HE WOULD BRING Me OUNCES OF POWDER FOR $900.00 An OUNCE. I WOULD BLOW HALF of THE DOPE TRYING TO COOK IT UP. I WOULD TAKE SMALL QUANTIITES to my Aunts house to let her Cook it into A Rock Form. Afterwards, We Would sit upstairs in her house and Smoke the night Away.

One night, I Entered her house With an eight ball of Powder Cocaine. My Auntie made A PROMISE Saying' . . . Peanut," After we Finish Smoking this Eight ball Up, Let's Quit this shit, and get OUR lives together.

Let's go Back to School, and get back on the right track, OKAY? I said, Yeah, Yeah, let's Finish Smoking, and that's it For Me. After We Finished Smoking all of the cocaine, My Auntie gave me all her pipes & Smoking Utensils to throw away. I left My Aunts house with the Paraphernalia. Those Words Stayed Glued to my Ears, So after leaving her house at 3:30 A.M. On my motorcycle I threw the box of Pipes on the Side of the Road, and Continued on my Way back to the Razzle Dazzle. I had tears in my Eyes but at the Same time I was HAPPY about quitting! As soon as I got back home, I tried to Rest My Head and Put the Past Behind Me. The Thoughts of Leslie & The Kids, The Thousands of Dollars I Blew on Cocaine, The Good times I had in the RAZZle DAZZle, Etc, I fell to Sleep on the Front Porch in Misery.

That Morning My Beer & Liquor Customers woke Me up Wanting there Usual drinks before they Went to Work. I Served them their drinks of beer & Liquor. I Was at THE HOUSE ALONE, SO I DECIDED to Count the Money Under the mattress. IT WAS SHOCKING HOW QUICK MY MONEY Disappeared. I COUNTED $250.00 DOLLARS, I WAS AT ROCK BOTTOM. ON TOP OF THAT, I WAS GETTING two lbs., fronted to me from my Connection in Charlotte. I owed him $1300.00 Dollars. I couldn't believe how I put myself in debt like that. So I went for broke, Took the $250.00 & the $52.00 in the Kitchen cabinet I made From Selling Alcoholic Beverages and Combined It to Buy An Eight ball For $300.00 dollars. After receiving the Eight ball from an unknown Source, I Quickly Rode my Bike to my Aunts House for her to cook the Powdered Cocaine.

As soon as She Answered the door I told her to cook up the Eight ball. She Said, "Peanut" Didn't I tell you I was Quitting. I'm going to beauty School to get My life together Boy! Plus I gave you you the Pipes, & Stuff last-night. Those words hit me hard. I had no intentions She was Serious about Quitting'. (She was Dead Serious.) My Aunt Even showed me books that She bought to Start Beauty School. Once I saw the books on the table, that let me Know how Serious She was. The next Words the Came from her Mouth . . .

So . . . When are you going to Quit? huh! huh! I Didn't know How to Answer, so I Said, Soon . . . and Rode Down the Road trying to think Where I Thew the Pipes & utensils She gave me to throw away. But I Completely Forgot Where the hell I threw them. So I Rode BACK to the house, locked the doors and tried to cook the powder Myself! I completely

Messed up the Dope. I Forgot to Put baking Soda With the Powder Cocaine, So I completely Ruined my Chances of trying to get High or Sell Cocaine. Now, I WAS TOTALLY BROKE, WITH NO Money, No Reefer NO Leslie, Etc. SO I HAD one LAST CHANCE, "FAT CAT". Hopefully he Should have some Money left. I Caught up with him that night But it was to late. He was in the Same boat as Me., Between My brother and I, WE MESSED UP ALMOST $51,000.00 Dollars in three months,. Now I Was in Big trouble, I Owe my Connection $1300.00 and He was Pissed! I Decided to Admit myself in a Rehab Center to get My life Back together. Plus It was a nice hiding Place from My Connection

I Stayed in the rehabilitation Center For 2 Weeks to escape the Danger of being Killed by My Powerful Connection. But they Called My Aunts House, Wanting Me to Bring My Motorcycle to them Until I PAY MY DEBTS. THEY GAVE ME TWO HOURS TO GET THE MOTORCYCLE TO THEM. I HAD MY MOTRCYCLE IN their GARAGE WITH in ONE 1 HR, 20 Minutes. MY REEFER CONNECTION WAS VERY VERY POWERUL, SO IF I DIDN'T WANT TO BE DUCK TAPED & CABLE ROPED, IT WAS BEST TO FOLLOW THER COMMANDS. THESE PEOPLE WERE NO one TO PLAY WITH. SO NOW, I WAS OUT OF A MOTORCYCLE. I STARTED SELLING My FURNITURE OUT OF THE RAZZLE DAZZLE TO SUPPORT MY DRUG HABIT. THE NEXT THING I LOST was THE RAZZLE DAZZLE! MY BROTHER "FATCAT" MOVED BACK HOME WITH MY STEPFATHER. BUT I CONTINUED TO LET THE STREETS BEAT ME DOWN. I COULD HAVE EASILY WENT BACK HOME TO LIVE WITH MY AUNT BUT I CHOSE TO LIVE THE STREET LIFE, NOW I'M LIKE A DOPE fiend ON THE STREETS CHASING A HIGH I'LL never Catch. I WOULD BORROW MONEY FROM GUYS TO GET BACK ON MY FEET. I WOULD MESS UP THEIR MONEY on DOPE, and DODGE THEM FOR MONTHS. I WAS FLAT ON My FACE AND I NEEDED HELP BADLY, BUT HOW CAN SOMEONE HELP YOU, IF YOU WONT HELP YOURSELF. I WOULD GO BY MY AUNTS HOUSE TO CHECK UP ON HER TO SEE IF SHE STARTED BACK SMOKING ROCKS, BUT TO NO AVAIL. I STARTED SMOKING in 1984-85

And here IT is going on 2001, Writing how long I WAS SMOKING CRACK FROM 84 to 98. I Blew Fourteen Years of My life Chasing a High I NEVER Caught. And I'm Truly proud to SAY this About MY Lovely

Auntie, Ms. Jacqueline A. JACKSON. She Quit Smoking Cocaine in 1989, SHE GOT HER beautician's License. SHE Now owns A BEAUTY SHOP in HER HOME in EAST SPENCER N.C. I LOVE YOU!!!

BUT UNFORTUNATLY, I'M IN PRISON WRITING THIS BOOK ABOUT MY mistakes OF NOT LETTING THE DRUG-LIFE GO. HOPULLY THIS BOOK ABOUT MY LIFE ON THE PIPE WILL TURN OTHERS AROUND, AND help them PERSUE a CAREER of the finer things in Life besides the DRUG Life.

Living my Life on the Pipe Almost Cost me my life. For Robbing DRUG DEALERS, Stealing, And Getting Robbed. Not to mention being shot 11 times, stabbed 3 times, and hospitalized due to overdose. Most of all, The DRUG Life Made me a Damn Fool.

One NIGHT I Was APPROACHED by a 400 lb. White Woman Who Offered me $700.00 DOllARs TO have Sex with her. I Asked her Did She have the money on her. She replied to me that She would have the Money as soon as the Mail-Man ran in the Morning, so I quickly went home with the Fat White woman. I made her take a bath while I waited in her bedroom until She Returned. When She Entered the room, She was Wearing a Silk Blue Thong. Now, Can You imagine a 400 lbs. white Woman in a thong. (Picture THAT OKAY!) The more I looked at this woman, the More I Wanted to say . . . You big heifer You can Keep that damn $700.00 dollars, but my drug habit was Calling. I took off my Clothes, put on a Condom and Put a Pillow over My Face. As she began to get on top of me, A THOUGHT CROSSED MY MIND . . . OH SHIT? SHEs going to BREAK BOTH OF MY DAMN LEGS. BUT TO MY SURPRISE, SHE WAS Light as a feather. I wanted this woman to get It Over With and get the hell off of Me. She Continued to Ride Me for hours. Suddenly She started breathing' like a Bull elephant. The Whole damn bed Shook when this Woman Started to have her orgasm. I Quickly took off the condom and ran in the bathroom to wash Myself off. When I returned to the bedroom, She was lying on the Right Side of the Bed Smoking a marlboro. I couldn't believe What I had done. I said to myself . . . DAMN! I Just had Sex with a Killer whale, But I got back in bed with her. I however turned my back to her because I didn't want her big ass Kissing all Over me and fell Straight to Sleep.

Suddenly, It WAS the next DAY! I Slept all that Morning, then I turned over to see Where the hell I WAS at, I noticed She was combing her long black Witch hair and She broke the Silence by Saying . . . get up baby! "The mail-man has came." I just about broke my damn neck getting out of that Big Ass bed. I Put on My Shoes, because I had already Put back on my pants that night, in case she asked me to have sex With her again. I was ready to go to the bank and get Paid. When We left her house, I was so damn excited I was all over that BIG WHITE WOMAN. HELL, She was trying to drive, But I WAS SNUGGLED UP BETWEEN HER, and THAT DAMN CHECK! As we Pulled up to the Bank, She ask me if I wanted to go in with her. I said, NAW, I'll wait in the CAR Until you get back. Within 5 Minutes, SHE CAME WOBBLING TO THE CAR WITH A BANK ENVELOPE. SHE GOT IN THE CAR AND COUNTED OUT 7 Hundred dollars, and Put It in my hands. I had no Choice but to Kiss her. I felt so damn good! I Even conned-the Woman to Buy me Clothes With the Money She Still had in the Bank Envelope. She Spent two-Hundred dollars on me at the Mall, Yes, I was even hugging' Her Big ASS in THE MALL in front of all those Beautiful Black sistas.

BUT I DIDN'T CARE, I WAS $700.00 Dollars Richer with $200.00 Dollars worth of new Clothes. We drove back to her house so I Could Change Clothes and take a Shower.

Afterwards, I was in a hurry to hit the Streets of East Spencer N.C. I felt I was on top on top OF The World Again.

After leaving The White Woman's House and being on the Streets of East Spencer, I felt so good, I wanted to go Clubbing' out of town and feel like My Ole Self Again. I Avoided the drug dealers, and Caught a cab all the Way to Lexington N.C. To the "Bow-Knots."

This was the Same Night Club where I jumped on my half-brother (Ronnie Joe). The Club was in full-Swing when I Arrived. I had the cab driver to drop me off at the Store Across the Street from the "Bow-Knots." I Pimped Across the Street to the "Bow-Knots". I strutted Across the Street to observe the beautiful black Chicks that were hanging outside the Club. I Could Sense they were Checking Me out. So I Really Started Pimping. I WAS Pimping so hard, you would have thought one of my legs was Shorter than the other.

So I pimped to the door of the "Bow-Knots" and Pulled Out My Bank-Roll that consisted of Six one-hundred Bills, and four twenty Dollar

Bills. I had Seven One-hundred dollar Bills before I Paid the cab driver his Fee. He charged Me $20.00 for his Services. As I Stood in the door-Way of the "Bow-Knots" to Pay the Door-Man, I had a better View of the inside of the Club. There were about 25 ladies waiting on the men to arrive, So guess who was the first Man. (yeah, You guessed it.)I reached into My Back pocket to flash My Money Once Again.

To impress the ladies that were behind me waiting to get IN, I peeled off a Hundred dollar Bill and held it out to the door-man. He replied "Now you know damn well I Ain't Got no Change this DAMN Early."

So I Quickly grabbed The Hundred-Dollar Bill from his hand, and gave him a twenty Dollar Bill. I Could hear the Young ladies behind Me Saying . . . "Damn, Baby You holding". I took my time getting the Change from the door Man Because "ALL eyes were on Me," and I LOVED IT!

So I Stuck My Fat Bank Roll in My front Pocket, Pimped Across the dance floor and Made my way to the bar To order a Whiskey Sour, & A Michelob Beer from the Beautiful bartender. I Extended a One Hundred Dollar Bill to Impress her also. To My Surprise, she Accepted the hundred-Dollar Bill and Changed it.

As I Was receiving the Change from the Young lady behind the bar, I noticed a gorgeous dark skinned Woman on the other Side Observing Me. I had a bad habit of eyeing other Women down, until they looked away first!

We stared at each other eye to eye for almost 30 Sec. before her eyes turned away from me. If I would have looked Away first, I Would have been the Weaker One. So I Continued to Stare at her and Sip My whiskey Sour. I Could sense Shyness in this beautiful queen, So I felt dominate over her. But I had to play my cards just Right! I moved towards her with Confidence To Break the Silence. Hello Ms. Lady, Could I buy you A Drink. I Said it in my Sexiest Voice. "Sure" She replied. I QUICKLY Snapped my fingers at the BARtender To Order the Lady the Same thing I was drinking. I gave the Bartender a twenty dollar Bill and told her to Keep the Change. She Smiled at me in surprise.

She Quickly Stuffed the remaining Dollars in her well developed breasts and Continued serving drinks to Other Customers. I turned my attention back towards the nice looking lady I was Standing beside. Well Ms, lady, Since I bought you these two drinks. I WAS Hoping you'll give me a dance in return. "Yeah," I guess I Can Do THAT, SHE SAID in a low Sexy Voice.

OO Oh No! "I'm not talking about dance to a Fast Record. I'm talking about Dancing to Something slow & Mellow baby." Do you think you can handle that! I replied,
"Yeah, I guess I Can," she said. As She dropped her head, and Continued to reveal her Beautiful pearly Whites.

Thoughts were running through My head. I had to think of a way to get the D. J's attention, So I told the Beautiful Lady to watch My Drink until I Use the Rest Room. I Pimped around the Corner towards the Bathroom only to go to the D.J. Booth. I Extended My hand toward him with A five Dollar Bill and Said. Yooo", My Man, Play me something nice & Slow Bro.

He Quickly Snatched the Money and started Digging through Albums. He held up the Album and said, I gotcha BRO! As I Walked against the Side of the Wall back towards the Restrooms, The Slow Mellow Music flowed from the Speakers bouncing off the Walls. THE D.J. Played Exactly What I Wanted to hear, A Slow Mellow Record by Prince, Called "Do ME BABY"! As I Approached the Beautiful DARK-Skinned lady, She was Sipping' on the Whiskey Sour daiquiri I bought her. I gently touched her on the Shoulder and Said, "damn" baby! Looked like they're playing My favorite Song. WHATS UP SEXY? "I said in a low Whisper," She gently grabbed my hand, and Walked to the Middle of the dance floor Staring me directly in the eyes with the Sexiest look on her face. She put her arms around my neck and Pulled Me Very Close to her, While I grabbed the Cheeks of her ass, and grinded to the record. We Stared at each other for the longest. We were in our on little world on the Middle of the dance floor. I Whispered Softly in her EAR! "So, you wanna tell me your name Now, OR later" "MARYANN", SHE said in a Soft Whisper.

"So Mary Ann," Can I go home With you", and have bacon & Eggs early in the morning?, I replied! My Words caught Mary Ann off guard, But to My surprise, She paused in the Middle of the dance floor, gently grabbed my hand and Said, "Yeah! Come on." She led me off the dance floor, Still holding my hand Walking towards the Exit door. She Completely forgot about our Beverages at the bar. But it was all good, I Said to myself. Before I knew it She was unlocking the doors of her Car in the Bow-knots parking lot. Thoughts were running through My Mind . . . Pussy, Pussy, Pussy! She drove Silently to her apartment, her eyes glued to the road. So I quickly managed to get A few questions in before We arrived.

"Mary Ann", Do you have a Boyfriend? No, She Replied "Do you stay by yourself?". No, She Replied. Before I knew it we were getting out of her car and going into her Well furnished apartment.

As Soon as she stuck the key in the door, She told me to make Myself at home, and Quickly disappeared into the bedroom.

She left Me Standing at the front door. I followed her orders by Making Myself at home. I helped Myself to the refrigerator. I noticed about 5 BOXES of Cereal on top of the Ice Box, so that made ME pose another question. I yelled from the Kitchen . . . "MARY ANN, Do you have any Kids?" Yeah, But She's over her Grandmothers house, "SHE REPLIED!" So I grabbed a Big Salad bowl, and helped Myself to a bowl of Captain Crunch Cereal. I Continued to glance around the Well furnished apartment, Everything was neatly intact. She had Wall to Wall carpeting, A floor Model television, Expensive leather furniture, BRASS Tables & LAMPS, Exotic Plants & flowers, Etc. This was the Perfect getaway for Me. But my investigation Wasn't over. My final Destination Was the Bathroom. I said to Myself . . . If Mary Ann's Bathtub & toilet is Clean, "She's Clean"! So I eased My way to the bathroom. I Opened the door to the Bathroom. "Her Restroom Was Spotless," no Bathtub Rings, No Toilet Rings, or Sink rings. She had Matching towels and Beautiful Ceramic ornaments hanging on the Walls. "She Passed the test"!!! This Was a Clean & Well Kept female. As I WAS Coming out OF THE BATHROOM, Her bedroom Door Opened. When Mary Ann Came Out, She Was in a Blue Negligee, and Her hair was laid BACK behind her Small ears, which donned 2 big gleaming diamonds. Mary Ann, looked like an AFRICAN PRINCESS with her head held high.

I Observed her from head to toe. "My My My," look what the good Lord is giving to me for my Birthday, I replied.!

I gently picked Mary Ann up off her feet, CARRIED her to the bedroom, and laid her down gently on the Queen Size Bed. I Could Smell her Sweet Perfume on her Soft Body. I began to caress her with My lips and hands, Kissing & Blowing on her neck to arouse this African Queen. I Could hear her Moaning, her hips were Swaying up and down and side to side. My hands & Tongue were working together. Mary Ann Was on Fire. I gently Sucked her nipples as She began to Moan louder. My hands Rubbed up & Down her Smooth thighs, and gradually moved towards her Private.

The Closer I got, the More She would shut her legs. Suddenly, I reached Her Private and felt Something Out of the Ordinary. "It was a Maxi-Pad." I fixed My lips to say. "Mary Ann", are you on your period? "Yeah", She Said in a Soft Moan. I had made a Vow to Myself, never Mess With a Woman When She's on the rag. "My night was fucked up." I was ready for action, so I Continued to conversate with her through the Wee hours of the night Until We fell asleep in each others arms.

When Morning time arrived. I was Sleeping like A new born baby. I opened my Eyes, and saw Mary Ann Standing Over Me with a Beautiful Birthday card.

I Reached for the Card to Open it, and a twenty Dollar Bill fell out of it. I had Completely forgotten about My Birthday. But She didn't! Somehow, Mary Ann Slipped from My Embrace that Morning, and drove up town to Buy A Birthday card. I really Admired her for the little things She Did for me. I grabbed her playfully to Express My Gratitude, and kissed her lightly on the lips. Peanut, "who do you Stay with in Salisbury" she asked in a Concerned manner? I Stay with a friend—"Why"? Cause I want you to move in with me," She replied! "are you Serious Mary Ann"? UUM-hum!" Don't you wanna Stay with Me.?" She Replied. "Do you Really want me to?"! I Said with Concern. "Yeah Baby", I'll Even take you to Salisbury So you can pick up your Clothes. She Replied! Then She disappeared into the Kitchen and Came back with a breakfast plate. It Consisted of bacon & Eggs with grits & Biscuits including a tall glass of ice cold Orange Juice.

She Served this to me in bed. Hell, I THOUGHT I WAS in heaven, being Served, like a King. "Peanut," After you finish eating, we're going to go pick up your Clothes "she said. I finished eating the home Cooked Meal. She had the CAR Started & Ready, to go Pick up my Clothes in Salisbury. As we Started on our way to Salisbury, I Went in Deep thought thinking how I was going to get the new Clothes Out of the WHITE GIRLS HOUSE. I had to think of a good lie to tell her And "Quick", We were only a 1/2 Mile from the White woman's House.

I Sure as hell didn't want Mary Ann to Know I WAS Sleeping with a 400 lb. White Woman for Money, and a place to Stay.

So instead of telling MARY Ann to park in the White woman's drive-Way. I Told her to park on a back Road. that Way I could Run to the front door without them seeing each Other. When We arrived on the back Road, I told Mary Ann "I'll be back in 5 Minutes." I Quickly Ran up the hill in the back Yard of the White Woman's house. I glanced behind me to see if Mary Ann's car Could be Spotted by the White Woman. Half of the Car was Revealed, but I Couldn't See Mary Ann's face Sitting behind the Steering Wheel. So I Knocked on the White Womans door, hard & fast. I Could feel her vibration from the front porch, although the porch was made of Cement. The door Opened, and She Was standing in the door-way Smiling when she Saw My face. I Quickly Stepped forward to get Around her. "Baby", Guess What? I didn't give her time to guess. I Wanted those new Clothes and to get the hell out of there With Quickness before Mary Ann started Blowing the car horn. "I Found a job in Lexington", I said with Excitement! baby help Me PACK My Clothes, okay!". I noticed the Sad frown on her face, So I tried to Cheer her Up by Saying . . . baby I promise I'll Come See you Every Week and help with the bills as soon as I draw my first Check OKAY? "But I'll take you to work in Lexington baby, Please don't leave Me" She Said, with tears falling from her eyes. I was Timing Myself from the second I Entered the front door. I Was in her house about 4 minutes packing & lying at the Same time. Within 5 Minutes, I was on my way out the door with a Plastic Bag of brand-new Clothes She bought me the day before. I promised that White Woman I was Moving in with her, But After Meeting Something that looked 110 percent Better made me have a Change of heart. Plus I Wanted to Start a new life in Lexington N.C. As Soon as I hit the front door, I Struck out Jogging through her back Yard. I was about 5 yards From the CAR When I Yelled to Mary Ann . . .

"crank up the CAR Baby !". I looked over my Shoulder to See if I Could See the White woman and she Was standing on the front porch with tears running Down her ROSIE CHEEKS. I quickly got in on the Passenger Side of the CAR and Yelled . . . Okay BABY, BACK UP, BACK UP! I DIDN'T Want MARYANN To PUT THE CAR in DRIVE, CAUSE IF SO, SHE WOULD HAVE SEEN WHO I WAS STAYING WITH. Mary Ann probably thought I had robbed a damn bank The way I Rushed her to get on the Highway. She was Scared shitless Until We reached Lexington City Limits. I Could See a Sigh of Relief on her face. I'm Sure she Could See the Same Expression on my face Also.

It only took 45 Minutes to Pick up My Clothes and drive back to Mary Ann's House. I felt a Sigh of permanent relief once My Clothes were packed in the Closet of my new home. Everything was going great Until One day Mary Ann was preparing Supper for me in the Kitchen.

I lost my temper and threw a butcher Knife in the Kitchen Wall. Her eyes got big As a bullfrog, "She Said . . . "Baby What's Wrong"! "Bitch", I been with you for 3 days now, and you ain't gave me no pussy Yet!. "I want Some damn Pussy"! I said with Anger." OKAY BABY, LET ME GO TO THE BATHROOM TO SEE if I've Quit SPOTTING, SHE replied in fear. "Within 30 Seconds, She was back in the Kitchen Saying' . . . "OKAY PEANUT, I QUIT SPOTTING. Those were the magic words for Me. We went from the Kitchen to the bedroom to have rough Sex!!! I held a grudge against Mary Ann for Making Me Wait so long. Mary Ann was a Beautiful DARK Skin Woman with a Good heart, But she Couldn't take the Place of Leslie. My heart Still belonged to the TRUE LOVE of My life, But she was nowhere to be found. The Sex Sparks died between Me & Mary Ann. We went from Having Sex Everyday to Every other day to Once a Week.

One night I WAS lying on the Couch looking at Cable Television, when Mary Ann asked Me if She could go out to party with her girlfriends. I Said, "Yeah, Just as long AS you have your ass here by 1:30 A.M.

SHE agreed To be in before 1:30 A.M, So she took off with her girlfriends to the "Bow-Knots". Soon it would be 1:30 A.M. I Wanted to see if Mary Ann really Obeyed My Command. Suddenly, I heard a CAR door slam. I glanced at the Clock, it was 1:25 A.M. I heard the Storm Door Open, She Stuck her Key in the door to let herself in the house. I was still in the Same Position, lying on my stomach on the Couch. When

she entered the living room, She was feeling pretty tipsy from drinking . . .
"Yeah baby, did you Miss Me?",She replied in a Sluggish Manner. "Yeah, I
See you brought your ass in before 1:30" I replied (In a sarcastic manner).
She staggered in my direction, and fell on My lower back and "farted right
on me". Sparks flew from my Eyes With Anger. "She totally Disrespected
Me". Out of all my years being around women, "never in My LIFE had A
woman farted in my presence."

She busted out laughing' as if it was funny! I quickly lifted Mary Ann
off my back and Cursed her ass out! After Cursing her Out, I Told her to
iron Me A pair of jeans, BECAUSE I'M GOING OUT! "SHE TRIED To
PLEAD HER CASE OF BEING SORRY, but She had drawn the last Straw.
IT WAS My TIME TO GO OUT CLUBBING AT THE Bow-Knots.

Mary Ann & I had Stayed together A Month and a half and already, I
was getting' tired of her. I WAS DRUG-FREE Living in LEXINGTON
N.C. I STILL MANAGED TO HOLD on To $300.00 OF THE MONEY
THE WHITE WOMAN had given ME. MARY ANN SUPPLIED MY
NEEDS FOR EVERYTHING. There was no need to Spend any Money.
I wasn't Buying any cocaine. So I Put on My Clothes that Mary Ann had
ironed for me and Walked to the Club. It was About 2:15 A.M When I
arrived at the Bow-Knots. The Club was in Full-Swing. But first I Wanted
to get My drink on before I got my groove on dancing' & flirting with
other women. I entered a boot-leg liquor house before partying. There
were beautiful Women Everywhere. The good thing about it was, I Didn't
Know any of them & they didn't Know Me, OR whom I was dating.

As I walked towards the liquor house, I noticed a Beautiful Red-bone
Standing on the Porch of the liquor house drinking a Miller's beer from a
bottle. I stared her Straight in the eyes to test who was the Weakest between
Me & her. We Stared each other in the eyes for A Minute, But She never
dropped her head, nor did She look away!! Finally the Contest was over. I
dropped My head and eased my way into the liquor-house. Never before
had a woman made Me drop My head, OR look in Another direction. I
WAS THE ONE FEELING WEAK And SHY! When I Walked past her, I
glanced Over My Shoulder to See if She was still Staring in My direction.
"Yep", SHE was still STARING! SO I ORDERED ME A COUNRY
CLUB BEER TO BUILD My COURAGE UP. I drank THE BEER
BEFORE I Left the BAR. Now I WAS READY FOR THE ULTIMATE

TEST. I Walked towards the front door to Stare that beautiful Ass Red-bone down!!!!

As I approached the front door, She had her back turned. I eased the door open to Catch her off guard. I grabbed her from behind, using My Sexiest Voice . . . "can I go home with you so you can make me breakfast in the Morning?" No . . . Because you talk to Mary Ann", She replied, in a Curious manner!

"So, what does Mary Ann have to do with you & Me" I-replied! "Nothing! Nothing at all! Come on . . . SHE replied in a flirtatious Manner. She quickly grabbed My hand And led the Way towards her apartment. I Asked," what's your name? "Pam," SHE replied in Return. Pam was a Beautiful Red-bone about 5'10" 29 yrs. Old with DARK brown Eyes, very Bowlegged with a Sexy Walk, and had a Beautiful Smile with a Silver tooth. She Seemed like the perfect Woman to take the place of Leslie.

As we entered her apartment, I felt a sigh of relief because I didn't know if Mary Ann was on the hunt looking for Me or what! I observed the apartment Closely and noticed how Well-Kept her Small apartment was. Nice paintings hanging' on the walls, Wall to Wall carpet, a nice Stereo System, Brass & Glass with Matching lamps. Etc. I managed to Make My Way to the bathroom to See how Clean it was. Pam's bathroom was so clean you could Eat food off her toilet Stool Seat, and I'm not Saying' that for a laugh "She was very clean!"

When I Came out of the Restroom to Check for filth, She was Sitting Indian Style on The living Room floor, listening to a group called "Surface". the name of the record was . . . "only you can make me happy"!

I set Right beside her in Indian Style as well. She looked me straight in the eyes and Started Singing to Me. I was amazed how much her features Resembled Leslie, "Even her Voice Sound like Leslie's", I was in a trance staring at the Beauty She Possessed. The only thing different between the two was their Skin Complexion; Leslie was pecan tan, and Pam was a Red-bone. As soon as the Record went off, I lifted Pam off her feet and walked her to the bedroom and had Sex for 2 hrs. She tried to make me stay Until Morning, But I had to Answer to Mary Ann. So I Kissed Pam on the Cheek and Walked My Way back towards Mary Ann's house. Pam and Mary Ann Stayed two Blocks from each other So I didn't have to far to walk.

As soon as I Approached the door Mary Ann Snatched it Open. She Asked . . . "where have you been Baby" I said, "at the Club . . . WHY?" SHE Said, "Baby, I came there looking for you But I couldn't find you". I said "I saw you, But I didn't bother to Say Anything,"—"Mary ANN. I Didn't Appreciate you disrespecting me by farting on my back. So don't let that shit happen again! OKAY".

SHE said "OKAY BABY—, I wont let it happen anymore"
Baby I have your Bath water waiting for you—please Hurry and come make love to me, please . . .

Now here I was. I just finished having Sex with Pam and now Mary Ann wanted to do the Same thing with Me. After taking a bath, I performed Sex with Mary Ann. She couldn't tell the difference cause I used an Excuse Saying' I was tired & Sleepy.

One Week went by, when I was Sitting at the house looking At Television with the front door open. I noticed a Man approaching the storm door "Knock, Knock, Knock".

Mary Ann was in the bedroom Cleaning & Dusting the house. The strange Man and I Stared each other Down. So I Call Mary Ann from the bedroom to Answer the door. "Mary Ann, Mary Ann, Some man is knocking on the door". She Stared at the strange Man from the living Room and replied! "I Don't Know him". I said, "Hell, I don't know him Either". She Opened the door, and Asked him, may I help you?" He replied "Yes, I'm looking for "Peanut". Mary Ann quickly turned on her heels, and Motioned Me to the door. I arose from the Couch to see what this Man Wanted. He motioned for me to Step Outside to talk privately. I stepped outside and Closed the Storm door behind Me. He said . . . "Peanut", Pam sent Me over here to come and get you", She Paid me Ten Dollars to bring you back with Me. So I turned around to Call Mary Ann, then I made a lame Excuse about My Brother getting into a fight down the Street. She wanted to drive Me down the Road to Check up on him, But I told her I'll walk down the street and take care of the Situation. I quickly put on my shoes and walked down the street with the Strange acting Man.

We walked one Block before starting our conversation. I broke the Silence by Asking how did he Know about me and Pam?. He told me that was her sister!

We continued to walk to his sister's house. I learned How much his Sister talked about Me around him. I was curious about her telling him about us having Sex. But I kept my Comment to Myself! As we Approached Pam's Front door, He tried to get Me to go in first. "I told him to go in first". We argued back & forth about who was going in the house first. The apartment was dark. Thoughts Ran across My Mind of getting robbed, or Busted in the head, so I insisted that he go in first. He finally gave in and entered the apartment first. I followed Suit behind him. After I Shut the door the lights came on.! People Jumped from behind doors & Walls yelling . . . "surprise!" "surprise! I was scared shitless, But After seeing the beautiful Women and noticing the beverages & food. I Came to My Senses. Pam had tried to surprise me with a get together party. Everyone was Cheering & dancing. For what Reason I Don't Know! As I observed all the beautiful ladies around Me, I Couldn't figure out which one was Pam So I asked her brother to point her out. He Said, She drove down by the Club looking for you, and that she would be back Shortly, So I Continued to help Myself to the expensive beverages she had at the house until she arrived. Suddenly the door Opened, and there She was! She was looking gorgeous as ever. Pam was the type of Woman who could Change her Appearance. She did not look like the same woman I had sex with last week.

As she stood in the doorway staring me up & down! I could see this woman Really had Strong feelings for Me, and I was feeling the same. I broke the Silence By Saying . . . "So you did all this for Me?", "Yeah!" She said in a shy manner "Well", I Hope this party you threw for Me doesn't last All night because I need Some private time with you Ms. lady". She blushed like a Childish girl. When she heard those words the surprise party lasted almost 3 hours. Everyone was feeling pretty tipsy when they left Pam's apartment.

As Pam and I started Cleaning Up the Kitchen & living room, I Could think back to when we had Sex for the first time. It was just a one-night stand. I thought no more about Pam. I thought it was over. But I guess she saw something Else in me! Finally We finished cleaning her apartment. She disappeared in the bedroom and when Pam re-appeared, She was wearing a Soft Pink Negligee, with her hair tied up in a Stylish fashion. She glided across the floor to approach me with her hands extended as if She wanted Me to Sweep her off her feet. I was in a daze looking at the beauty this woman held. The fancy hair Style, The Sexy negligee, The Soft Red-Skin, The Bed-Room Eyes. But most of all She had the prettiest little feet. her Smile stole the Show, she had sparkly white Even teeth with a silver tooth in the front.

Now I wanted to make this woman my "Main Woman". Even if It takes breaking up with Mary Ann.

(THE END OF VOL I PRINT)

A portrait of Queen Sheeba a virtuous woman.

If my deceased father had a long lost twin it would have been Richard Pryor.

VOLUME 2

AT THE AGE OF 27, Things were going in My favor with the Beautiful BLACK Women in Lexington N.C. Pam & I had just finished making passionate love, as we laid in her Queen size bed Smoking cigarettes exhausted from making wild passionate love. I posed a question to Pam. Pam how would you feel if I asked to move in with you", She said, "Baby, how are you going to do that, You're staying with Mary Ann?". I replied "tomorrow morning when I take Mary Ann to Work. I'll have the car, So I'll take my clothes from her house, and move them here". Pam stood up from the bed in her birthday Suit, looked me directly in the eyes, Saying', . . . "Peanut, If you do that! I'll leave my house Key under the front Porch floor Mat, Plus I'll leave $20.00 with the Key", I was so excited from hearing the magic Words. I Hopped out from the covers and Started Putting on my Clothes in a hurry. I replied "Baby I promise I'll have my Clothes in this house before you get off work tomorrow Evening". She replied "OKAY-BABY I HEAR YOU TALKING. As soon as I was Completely dressed, I planted a passionate Kiss of assurance on Pam's lips that I would have My Shit out of Mary Ann's House & into Pam's apartment.

As I left Pam's Apartment walking towards Mary Ann's apartment. "I was feeling on top of the world. I felt as if Pam would take away the pains from the hurt of loosing Leslie. Now I was only a block away from the apartment of Mary Ann. I Had to think of Something quick, I could have Played the field with Both Women, But my heart wasn't with Mary Ann anymore. Pam had stolen that within a few hours! As I turned the Corner of the Street Mary Ann lived on, I Could See her Standing in the doorway looking for me. It was 3:45 A.M. I didn't realize how long I had Stayed over Pam's apartment (Almost 8 hrs.)

MARY ANN Spotted Me in the parking lot. She held the Storm door Open Until I Entered the apartment. I Could See that She had Worried herself crazy. She wondered if i got jumped on from the lame excuse I had given her about my brother fighting Down the Street. "Baby, are you okay?"—are you hurt? I replied "naw Baby, I'm alright, Me & My brother Beat the Shit out of those guys"! She disappeared in the bathroom to Run My bathwater. I Went to the bedroom to undress. When She came out of the bathroom she had a beautiful Smile on her face. I quickly Walked around her to Avoid her getting Close to me. I didn't want her to Smell the Clothes or myself. I had a Perfume Smell on My body from laying' Up with Pam, So I Quickly Shut the bathroom door, and stepped into the Bathtub. I had a bad habit of locking Bathroom doors when I'm not around a woman.

AS I Was lying in the Semi-Hot bathwater I began to Relax my mind, My thoughts began to drift off into Space "Damn,—Peanut this is your last-night laying in this bathtub";

This is your last-night at this house, So FUCK her one more time And then burn the Road up"! My thoughts were Running a Mile a Minute! I Was thinking about My future with Pam, And How different things would be. I thought about Leslie and her Two Boys, Hoping I would Someday return home And She'll be around waiting. My thoughts were interrupted by Mary Ann . . . "Baby—Do you want me to come in, and wash your back,?" She replied in a Concerning Manner.

"NAW—babe, I'll be out in a few Minutes." As I Started drying Myself off with the towel, She Knocked on the door and said "I need to use the bathroom." As I Opened the door, She quickly Unzipped her Pants to take a Piss. She Stared Up at me, and Said . . . "Baby—I love you!" The words Caught Me off guard. I Could See her from the Corner of my eye. she was waiting on Me to Say those Same Words to her, But I Couldn't repeat them; my heart wasn't there. So I Quickly Changed the Conversation asking her to wash out the Bathtub for me. I Walked into the Bedroom to get Some Rest.

I laid on my side of the bed With my back turned towards the Wall. I Could hear MARY Ann Running the Water to Rinse out the tub. She was in a good Mood humming & Singing etc.

When She came into the bedroom, She Was Wearing a long T-Shirt, With nothing on underneath. As She laid beside Me, She Started Kissing My Neck, and caressing my Shoulders. This told Me She Wanted to have Sex. "Baby, Make love to Me"! She replied in a Soft Whisper. I Continued to Play Asleep. I began to snore AS She Started licking all Over My Neck, slowly Moving Down to My CHEST! SHE Rolled ME FLAT On My BACK, And proceeded in a Downward Manner. I had never had Oral sex, So I Continued to Play Sleep TO See how far She Would go. I noticed She Stopped Kissing & Licking on My Chest. So I Opened My Eyes to See What Was the Hold-Up. She was taking off her nighty T-Shirt She Wore to bed. When She looked at me I Quickly Shut my Eyes as if I WAS ASLEEP. I Could feel her getting on Top of My Body. Now She was Kissing my neck. Again . . .

She gently eased beside me, laid flat on her back in her birthday Suit, and Rubbed me on my Shoulder, only to Say . . . "Baby, It's your turn . . ." DO ME . . .

I said, "Bitch", you must be CRAZY in the head"!

I Wasn't down with having Oral sex, let alone With a Woman whose history I didn't know. She Continued to beg Me to go down on her, But I had My Mind Made UP! NO NO NO . . .

So I Pretended like I had a terrible headache Saying . . . "Mary Ann—Baby Could you bring me a Couple of aspirin for a Head-Ache?" She Went to the Medicine Cabinet in the bathroom, came back with 2 aspirins & A glass of Water. She Extended her hand as I grabbed the medication, and I took the aspirin, and fell to Sleep with My Back turned to the Wall.

Daylight finally crept through the bedroom Windows As I began to Open My Eyes. The Thoughts of Moving in with Pam were Clear on My Mind as I got up to take a Hot Shower.

Mary Ann was Still Sleeping Peacefully in the bedroom. When I finished ironing Clothes for the both of US. I prepared breakfast around 10:30 P.M. I fixed her favorite breakfast grits & Eggs with Country Ham & Biscuits. She was Surprised to get breakfast in bed. "MARY ANN—Wake Up baby," its time to Eat"! "What time is it Baby.?" She replied "It's time to get Up." I replied. I had her bath Water waiting, Plus her work Clothes ironed Out. After her taking a bath & brushing her teeth, eating breakfast and Cleaning UP. It Was Almost time for her to go to Work. She didn't have to be at Work Until 3:00 P.M. But I made Up an Excuse Saying I had to Use the CAR to go to Salisbury to handle Some business. It was about 2:05 P.M. and She Was in the Bathroom putting on Make-Up, When She heard the CAR horn Blowing for her, BUMP! BUMP!! BUMP!!

I had the Car Started ready to take her to work earlier than usual "damn, baby! I Don't have to be at Work Until 3:00 o Clock" She yelled in a Smart Manner,

"Yeah Baby, i know this but I got Some business to handle at 3:00 o'Clock," I replied

When She Came out to the car ready and dressed for Work, I Quickly back the CAR out of the drive-Way and drove about 45 MPH. Through Town, trying' to beat the School buses before the Kids got Out of School. Within 10 minutes. She was Walking through the doors of her job. I Watched her body fade in with the Rest of the Employees. As I drove from the Curve, I said to Myself . . . "Well, That's the last of Seeing her"

Within 20 minutes I was back at Mary Ann's apartment, Packing My Clothes and Putting them into the CAR. I Could hear her Very last Words As She got out of the CAR. "Baby, Don't Forget to Come Pick Me Up at 11:00 o'Clock." I had no intentions of Picking Mary Ann up from Work. My intention was to leave the Car in the drive-Way at her apartment With the Keys in the ignition Switch. As I drove away from the apartment, I thought about the 2 page letter I just finished writing her, telling her how Sorry I Was for not being able to Pick her Up from Work, and I Went back to Salisbury to Stay With My Mother because She was Sick and Didn't Want to be at the house alone.

Hopefully She Would forgive me for that pitiful excuse of a lie, little did She Know that I Would be Staying only 2 Blocks from her apartment. As I Entered the drive-Way of Pam's apartment, I noticed a nosy neighbor from Up-stairs. She Watched me carefully as I got out of the car to Check Under the Porch floor-Mat. When I Raised the Mat Up, I Saw a 20 Dollar Bill With a Key wrapped inside the Money. I Quickly Unwrapped the Key, Stuck the Key in the door and turn the knob. "Bingo"! I Quickly took the Key Out, and Opened the door. I Went to the CAR for My Clothes and Carried them In the house. When I Walked back to the Car and Started It, I noticed the Young nosy lady Up-Stairs "Still watching Me" As I drove Mary Ann car back to her apartment. I got Out of the Car and Walked 2 Blocks back to Pam's Apartment. When I Entered the Apartment I felt a Sigh of Relief as I begun to hang up My Clothes Right beside Pams.

To My surprise I heard a door slam. "I Froze in my tracks" I heard footsteps Coming Closer& Closer towards the Walk in Closet. As I Stood in my tracks Motionless, I looked Up! It WAS Pam! She Was Smiling and Jumping Up & Down With excitement Showing on her face. oooh baby, "You did Move in With Me"! "Yeah, I told you I Was," We were hugging & Kissing One another for about 5 Minutes, So I decided to Put My foot down by Saying . . . "Baby, If you have a Boy-friend or a friend Boy, get Rid of him! Cause Its a new Sheriff in town, and I don't need no troubles

& heart-aches." She Said, "Baby, You don't have to Worry about that, I've lived the Single life for Years."

"Alright, I Don't Want Any TROUBLE NOW!" I Replied in a Concern ing manner.

Suddenly, I Heard a loud Knock at the front Door. Knock, Knock, Knock, Knock!!! You See!, "That's one of your Boy-friends Now. Go Tell that ASS-HOLE That it's a new Sheriff in town." As we Slipped from Each Others WARM Embrace, I hid behind the door to listen to the Conversation, to Make Sure She Would Run the guy away! When She Opened the door, I Heard a familiar Voice Coming from the Outside Saying . . .

Hello Pam, is Peanut Over here?"! I Was Scared Shitless! It was Mary ANN. I Continued to listen as I heard Pam Say . . . "Yeah, He's in the bedroom. Later on, I found out that the nosy Ass heifer Up Stairs from Pam's apartment, Called Mary Ann on her job and Told her I Was Putting Clothes in Pam's apartment. "I Wanted to Kick the Bitch's ass"! As I Heard two foot Steps Coming towards Pam's bedroom, MY Eyes got bigger than a Boe Dollar. Suddenly the Bedroom door Opened. Both women Came in, "Peanut, Mary Ann Wants you"! I Couldn't Even look her in the Eyes, I Was BUSTED!

"Baby, What are you doing over here" MARY Ann Replied! I looked up at Pam and She was looking at Me With her hands on her hips Waiting on an Answer.

"Go AHEAD"—Tell her Peanut, "Tell her why you're Over here" Pam said, in a sarcastic manner. I Wanted to tell her, "I Don't want you No-More," BUT THE WORDS WOULDN'T COME OUT!

Mary Ann grabbed My ARM and tried to yank me from the Bed, But I quickly Snatched away from her embrace Saying . . .

"Mary Ann, I Don't Want you No-MORE, This is Where I Wanna be," She Couldn't believe What She Was hearing. So She tried to grab me once again, I yelled at her Saying . . . "I Don't want You, I LIKE Pam"

SPARKS Shot from Mary Ann eyes, never before have I Seen her like this. She Said, "Come and get the rest of Your Shit Out of My CAR." You See, I Managed to leave a Couple Sets of Clothes in the trunk of Mary Ann's CAR, just in Case things didn't go Right Between Pam & I. But She had discovered them, So I quickly got Up off the Bed and Walked to the CAR With Mary Ann to get the Remaining Clothes I had Stashed in her trunk. When Mary Ann Popped the trunk of the CAR, I Slowly Bent Under the trunk hood to gather My Clothes. Mary Ann was Standing Over

Me begging & Pleading with Me to Come back home With her. Pam was Standing in the door Way. I Wanted to impress Pam, so I Shouted at Mary Ann telling her "Girl I don't want you Any More, Can't you Understand that?," Fire Fell in Mary Ann eyes. My head Was Still Under the trunk of the CAR and Suddenly I noticed the trunk Closing in on the top of My head. But I Managed to escape the deadly Blow of the trunk. I Snatched My head back in the nick of time. But My Right hand Wasn't Quick Enough. Pain Ran Up & Down My ARM. Mary Ann had Slammed My finger in the trunk and jumped in the CAR, Started it, Put the CAR in drive and Pulled off With My finger trapped in the trunk of the Car.

I Was yelling & Screaming . . . "STOP BITCH," STOP STOP! The CAR Was building up Speed. I had two choices! Either get dragged down the Street, OR yank My finger out of the trunk. So I took a hard yank, and fell Running Down the Road. My Finger Was Completely Smashed!. Pain Exploded from my Hand. I Stopped to Examine My Right finger and realized My finger nail was Completely torn off. Mary Ann Continued to drive Angrily down the Road While Pam Stood in the door Way Showing Concern for me. I Slowly Walked back to Pam for Medical treatment. She took me in the House and bandaged My finger Up. As I looked Pam in her Eyes, I Said, "Well, babe It's Me & You," SHE is HISTORY! She looked Me directly in My Eyes and said, "Baby, I'm going to do everything In My Power to Keep you Happy. You don't have to work or pay any of the Bills, The Only thing I ASK of You is Have My Bathwater ready for Me When I get off Work & fix Me Something to Eat." Those Words Were Music to a free-loaders EARS After hearing her Request.

I Continued to get babied & pampered by Pam. I quickly walked to the bathroom to Run her Water in the tub While She Was in the Kitchen frying' Potatoes & Hot Dogs. After Eating & taking A bath together, We Started Playing' Some old school Albums She had for years. We listened to the Records of Johnnie Taylor—, "Who's Making love to your Ole lady"

Emotions—"Best of My love" Patti LA Belle—"If only you KNEW How much I NEED You", CLARENCE CARTERS—"STROKING," Minnie Rippleton—"Memory lane," Etc. We Stayed Up to the Wee-hours of the night Sipping' On E & J brandy, and Dancing to Slow Music. We found ourselves in bed making PASSIONATE Love together. My first Encounter having Oral sex Was With Pam, She Made Sounds Coming from her Mouth that I've never heard Until this very day. I didn't Know if

She Was In pain, or if it was her first Encounter having Oral sex Performed On her. I really didn't LIKE HAVING ORAL SEX, BUT I enjoyed HEARING HER SCREAM FOR MORE.

AFTER TWO DAYS OF LIVING UNDER Pam's ROOF, SHE LAID HER FOOT DOWN, "PEANUT—I DON'T MIND YOU SMOKING" Reefer in the house just don't have anyone in here When I'm At Work" "No PROBLEM" I said With assurance. Pam Would buy me $20.00 bags to Keep me at home, for Me to Smoke by Myself When She Was at Work (She Worked 2nd Shift,)

It WAS About 4:00 o'clock P.M. I WAS listening To Pam's FAVORITE Album SURFACE . . . "Shower Me With Your love." I Fired up a nice Fat joint. After Smoking half of the fat joint, I decided to Clean UP the house as Usual and take the trash out to the Dumpster. I Saw a Cool looking brother Walking Down the Street, So I Introduced Myself to him and he Said his name was Horse. I ASKed Horse did he Smoke Reefer? he Said "Hell Yeah"! So I Invited him in the house to Smoke a few joints and listen to Some Music. Well, after Smoking 2 OR 3 Hog leg joints I turned Up the Stereo system, to listen to the Instruments in the Go-GO Record "Sardines & PORK and Beans!" The Door flew Open! Pam was in the DOORWAY Holding a, .25 Automatic Nickel Plated Pistol. Her lips were moving, but I Couldn't hear her because the Stereo was Playing Wide Open. I Managed to Ease to the STEREO and Cut the Music down. The Words Came from Pam's Mouth Loud & CLEAR. "GET THE FUCK OUT MY DAMN HOUSE"! HORSE was Scared shitless & So Was I. We Both Jumped up from the Sofa and Rushed towards the door. Only one of us made it out the door. She Held the gun to my head and demanded that I Sit My ASS Down. I STARTED PRAYING to GOD, ALLAH, MOSES, MARY, EVERYBODY I COULD THINK OF, EVEN, "JEZEBEL"

"THIS BITCH IS CRAZY" I SAID TO MYSELF,"

"DIDN'T I TELL YOU NOT TO HAVE ANYBODY IN MY HOUSE" SHE Replied. "Pam—I thought you were talking about Women, I Didn't think you were talking about Guys too," I Replied in a nervous Voice. "I'm talking about Every damn Body, The guys only Want to Come in here to Scope out My damn house So they Can Come Back later on and rip me off" She replied.

I Was Staring down the barrel of a loaded gun. I put on my best Puppy Dog Face, and said "baby Listen, I'm sorry! I give You My Word This Will

Never HAPPEN again. Please Pam, Please put the gun down, Please Baby. After hearing Me beg for My life, I noticed the gun Was lowered From My face. The PLEADING WORDS were sinking HER. SHE Finally LOWERED THE GUN FROM MY FACE, AND SET IT on THE Coffee Table. It Was time to Make My Move, I jumped Up from the Sofa, pushed her against the Wall & slapped the Shit out of her. I Could See fear in her eyes as I Grabbed her by the throat and said "Bitch, if you Ever Put Another gun in my face, you better Use it."

I Could See the tears forming in her Eyes as I began to Put My meanest look on My face. She WAS terrified, I Couldn't Control My Anger. Suddenly, I Stood back and gave her a Chance to Pick up the Gun on the Coffee table. She was only inches away from it, But She wouldn't take that Chance. I Would have been on her Ass So Quick, She Wouldn't have Known What hit her.

You See, at the Age of 27, I WAS a STONE COLD Fighting MACHINE, BUT I WAS SENSITIVE WHEN IT came to hitting Women. I just wanted to prove to Pam that I was No SOFTY. After Kissing & Making up, I Questioned her. about how she knew I had Someone in her apartment?, She Said, The Girl from Up-Stairs Called her on the job, and Said I Had Some Guy in The apartment. Plus, She Complained about me Playing the MUSIC too loud. That nosy heifer reminded Me of Ms. CLARA that Played on BE-WITCHED. ALWAYS getting INTO OTHER Peoples business. Pam & I Made a Vow to Never argue, Fuss, Or fight again. After that, We Sealed Our Vows With Tattoos. I Wanted to Show how Much I loved her by Putting her name (Tattooed) on My Right arm. She also Did the Same, but on her Shoulder Blade instead. Even today I'm Wearing her name on my Right arm.

After 2 Months of living with Pam and Free-loading Etc. The land-lord came by for the Rent Money. Pam had Just got Paid, her pay-check was $237.00, and the Rent Was $225.00. I Remember Pam giving him the Whole Pay-Check. He Reached in his Pocket and gave her $7.00 and Walked Out the door. Pam fell on the Sofa and Started Crying. I said, "Whats Going on Baby"?! She Replied, "Peanut" . . . "I CAN'T DO THIS BY MYSELF, YOU GOT TO FIND A JOB."

After that, I knew My free-loading Days were coming to an End. That Very next day, Pam paid a beautiful Red-bone to take me Job Searching. She told me that She would Come by in the morning, and to be looking out for her in a Blue Escort, and her name was "Peaches". Well, Pam was working double shifts to make ends Meet. When I heard a Car horn outside of our apartment, I Took a peek out of the Window and Saw a Light Blue-Escort. I put on my best dress Pants & Silk Shirt to impress People on the Job Site. I had on my BLACK Stacy Adams, I was looking pretty damn good I Must Admit. I Walked to the mirror to take one last glance at myself. I Stepped out of the apartment Pimping to the CAR. As I APPROACHED the CAR and Opened the door to get in, I Bent down to Observe the driver. I was Stunned! This Woman Was Awesome and Very eye catching. She was High-Yellow with a Keen Pointed Cute nose, her eyes were Light green, and she had Beautiful White Teeth. She had Indian hair beyond her Shoulders. Baby Hair Ran down the Side of her face. I was Speechless When I Set in the CAR. "Hello . . . My name is Peaches! "Where do you Want to go First?" I Put on my Sexiest Voice and Said . . . "Anywhere Your beautiful little heart desires." She start Blushing from the Quick Response. As SHE Pulled out from the PARKING lot I noticed Ms. Clara Peeping out of her Kitchen Window, But the Bitch didn't have nothing to tell, Because Pam paid this Beautiful Lady to take me Job Searching. We drove To about 5 OR 6 Companies filling Out Job Applications. The More we Rode around, the More I got to Know this Beautiful Red-Bone. I Posed a Couple Questions to Peaches, "Peaches, are You From Lexington N.C.?" "No BABY, I'm FROM UP-STATE"! So You're not a Country Gal huh?! "It Depends on what You're talking About"! She Replied Well, Do you Enjoy Fishing? I Stated with Curiosity "Oh! Yeah I LOVE to Fish" SHE SAID IN an Exciting MANNER. "Damn Babe! I'm CRAZY about fishing"—"Do YOU PUT YOUR Worm on the Fishing hook by yourself"?, "Yeah! I Use Minnows, Crickets & Cut Baits." I was Amazed how a City girl Knew So much about Fishing, So I said," "Girl, one day we gotta go fishing together." She Said, "alright, But You can't let Pam Know about us going fishing, cause Pam's CRAZY"!

Those were the magic Words, Cause if She would Sneak off With Me Fishing, imagine what Else She would do behind Pam's back.

As we approached the City Limits, She invited me to go with her to a liquor house on the outer Parts of Lexington. I Agreed to go with her. I Wanted to be Under this beautiful Woman all day long. So we Drove up to A two-Story House with Cars Parked in the yard, on the Curve and in the drive Way. She Asked me if I Wanted to Come in. I Accepted her offer With Pleasure. She Asked Me did I Want anything to drink. I Said, "Peaches I Don't have any Money on me "Right Now! But" . . .

"Baby don't Worry about it, Pam gave Me $10.00 Dollars for gas. I already have a full-tank of gas. So I'll Buy the drinks"

As We Entered the nice looking liquor house, She ordered 2 cans of Malt Liquor Beer. Malt Liquor wasn't my type of Beer but Since she was buying; It Didn't matter!

After drinking the Malt Liquor, She Quickly ordered two More and drank them also. She Went for Round 3. I was feeling light headed, so I staggered my way to the CAR. 5 Minutes later She walked to the Car just as straight as when She Came. The Malt Liquor didn't Even effect her. This Fine Ass Woman Could hold her Booze.

She drove the CAR Away From the Curve, and proceeded to drive With Caution. We were less than 3 Minutes away from the apartment When Peaches made a Sharp Right turn heading toward her apartment, Crazy thoughts crossed My Mind! I said to Myself, If Peaches takes me to her apartment, Invites Me in the Place for Something, then She wants to have Sex with me. As we drove up in her Drive Way, She Cut the CAR off, and Said, "Peanut, You Wanna Come in For a Minute?, I gotta Use the bathroom"

Yes! Yes! Yes!. I Said in My Mind. Yeah, I need to use the bathroom too, I said in a relaxed way. As She Went up the Stairs to her apartment, I took Careful notice how her hips Swayed from Side to Side. that Ass Put me in a trance Switching back & forth. She Opened the door to her apartment And disappeared into the Bathroom. I Was left Standing around in the living Room observing my Surroundings. Her pad Was neatly intact. But Something Caught My eye in the living Room, More than Anything in her house. It was a Weight lifting Set in a Corner With almost 350 lbs. hanging on the bar. Thoughts Ran through My Mind . . . Now, I know damn Well that woman ain't lifting no 350 lbs. The Woman has a big Muscle bound Nigga Somewhere. My thoughts were interrupted by Peaches Walking from the Bathroom With her hair hanging' down to her ass. But Most of all, She was wearing Some Black & Pink Bikers that looked like Someone

Poured her into them. She Pulled her hair up, before She sat down With her legs gapped Open Right in front of Me! I Said To Myself, What is the Purpose of her Coming to her house, Changing' Clothes & letting her hair down and falling back on the Sofa with her legs spread Wide Open? The more I Stared between her legs, the More I began to Rise. I Could'nt help Myself For Jumping on top of her, Kissing all Over her neck, and Sucking on her nipples to arouse her. She Quickly Stopped me to invite me into her bedroom. Peaches Came out of those bikers, and stood naked before Me. My Penis Jumped to Attention as I got on top of her, and Rode her like a Wild Stallion. Peaches was 38 Years of Age, and Well experienced in having Sex. We continued to have Sex for One hour & 30 Minutes, When we heard a loud Knock at the door. She Slowly got off Of My Sweaty Body to Peep out of the Door. When I heard her Rushing back towards the bedroom Whispering . . . "Peanut-GET UP! PUT YOUR CLOTHES on, IT'S MY BOY-FRIEND." Again, I was Scared Shitless, the Only thing I Could think of Was the 350lb. Weights. IF THE BIG NIGGA CATCH ME in HIS House, he'll Snap my DAMN neck. "My Mind was Running a Mile A Minute." The thought of fighting this guy was Out of the Question.

"Baby, hurry up! Put on Your Clothes." She made it Seem like her Boy-friend was a Killer, and I wasn't about to test him. Peaches led me out of the Back door for Safety. I ran through yards & jumped fences trying' to Put Distance between Peache's apartment. Suddenly I found Myself Walking & breathing heavier than Ever on a back Road only a few Block from Pam's apartment. Finally I was at the front Door. As I Entered the apartment, I noticed everything was Exactly how I left it. No-one was Home]. As I began to wash Myself off in the Sink I Stared at Myself in the mirror, Saying' to Myself "peanut"—You're a bad Motherfucker". You fucked the Shit out that gal." Suddenly, I Walked out of the Bathroom to Change Boxers, when I noticed an eye Peeping' at Me from behind the Bed. "IT Scared the Shit out of Me". I Yelled in Fear of Someone breaking in. I screamed at the top of my lungs! She finally Came from behind the bed laughing & Picking. It was Pam!

HER Face Was a sigh of Relief, She asked me, "You fucked the Shit out of Who.?" "You Baby, I Was thinking about you Last night when we had Sex." THE QUICK thinking Paid off, as She begin to ask Questions about Me going Job Searching. I told her We drove to about 5 or 6 Job Sites to fill out Applications. Hopefully they'll Call if Any Openings come up.

That night I Escaped Death twice.

Another Month passed by living with Pam She was Still working Double Shifts, Carrying' the Work load by herself. I WAS in Desperate need of a job, So I began to go to the local Stores & Restaurants to Seek Employment. I was getting Temporary Jobs, Painting, Business Signs for Stores & Small Companies. Being A Naturally Born Artist paid off at times. But the Business wasn't Steady. One day I was Painting a food Sign, or Menu Sign for an old man named Nick. As I WAS Painting his Menu Sign in the Store, Nick noticed a black limousine across the Street From his Restaurant. Two black Guys Jumped out to Observe a Vacant Building. It was a Convenient Store that had been closed down for Almost six Months. This was the Same Store I parked My Motorcycle at When I Jumped on My Half-Brother (Ronnie-Joe). I noticed the black chauffeur as he Came in the Restaurant. He looked about 27 Years of Age, He was well-dressed but What Caught My Attention Was the Rattle Snake Boots he wore. We Spoke to Each other at a Distance. He ordered two Iced teas, and Walked back Across the Street to the Store. I noticed from the Window, that He was pointing at Me from across the Street. He was telling the expensively dressed Man Something about Me. Within Minutes Both Men were talking to Me Face to face about doing Work for them.

They introduced themselves as Chris & Fred! Chris Was the Limousine driver. He was light-Skinned, Well-dressed With a Jeri-Curl. At the time Jeri-curls were in Style.

He was about 5'll", With a deep Voice.

Fred Was the Money-Man. He had it all! Six Expensive CARS, 2 Motorcycles, A $950,000.00 dollar Home, and A Beautiful Woman for Every day of the Week Etc,.

Later on I found out that Fred's Mother Adopted Chris so Fred could have Someone to grow-up With. Chris was His Foster Brother! Fred broke the Silence by Asking . . . Yo, Peanut, if I have You a Wall Built on this premises, Would You be willing to Paint Me Something Extraordinary on it?" I Couldn't believe What I was hearing, but I Played if Calm. "Yeah But it depends"! On What!? He replied, "It depends on how Much Money we're talking." You See I Wasn't Sure whether this Guy was Bull-shittin me OR not! So I Wanted to Know if he was loaded, or if he was trying' to

Play A Big Willie OR Something. He wanted to See Some Art Work, and pictures I've done in the Past, So I invited them both to the apartment. They Accepted My invitation.

As I got in Fred's Limo! I Said to Myself . . . "Damn,-this guy can take my Financial troubles away if he's not Bull-Shittin' Around"! We drove away from the Closed down Convenient Store and headed towards Pam's apartment. I gave them the directions to get there. Within 2 Minutes, We arrived in the driveway. As always, that damn Ms. Clara Was Peeping' out her Kitchen Window when we Entered the apartment. I told Fred & Chris to wait in the living Room Until I came back With my drawings. When I came from the bed-Room With my paintings, Fred & Chris were staring at Pam's Picture on the Coffee table. Fred Said . . . "Damn Peanut"! I Know her, "that's Pam"! I've Fucked her, Ate her Pussy, and Everything"! I was Shocked with Anger.

I Wanted to Knock the Shit Out of him, But I remained Calm. I said, "Man! What Kind of Shit are you on? That's My Woman! One day I'm going to Fuck one of your ladies And throw those Same words in Your Face"! He Smiled SARCASTICALLY and Said, you can't Fuck My Women. Evidently this Fred guy didn't Know Me. he didn't know My reputation with Women. So I Extended my Paintings & drawings out to him. Fred & Chris were Shocked that I Could draw so good. So Fred said, "Damn! I Didn't think you could draw like that!" HE told me to meet him at 9:00 o'clock P.M. to Start Painting on the Wall he would build for me. Then he left. I had Told him that I Might Show up, and I might not. I WAS Still Pissed from the thoughts of Him having Sex with Pam. About 3 hrs. later, Pam Came barging in the door. I was sitting at the kitchen table waiting for her ass to come Home.

"Hey Baby", She Said with a Smile on her face.
What the hell are you doing Fucking Fred?—I asked with Anger in my Voice. Her Mouth Flew Open. She Said, Peanut, that's been 5 yrs. Ago. You wasn't Even in the Picture when I Met Fred."

"Well, why did you break up with him?"! "Because Fred's CRAZY" He wanted to Marry Me, But I didn't wanna get married then. Early that next day; I walked down to the Convenience store to get some kool aid. Once I got there I noticed that Fred had hired every wine'o in town to build a wooden wall. AS I approached Fred, he asked me where had I been, because I have been waiting on you. I thought he was bull shittin about building the wooden wall. He asked me what type of paint did i need to paint the wall? The wall was 12 feet high and 30 yards long, made out of treated wood. Fred hopped in his truck, went uptown to buy the paint and brushes. The total of the materials came up to $ 800.00. After we got all the materials in the truck, he asked me how much was i going to charge him to paint the wall. I told him I was going to charge him the same amount as the materials cost. Within 3 days I had the wall completed. To my surprise he PAID me on the spot. The wall drew so much attention, that the Winston Salem Journal came to interview me about the wall. They even put my picture in the paper beside the wall. The wall consisted of exotic animals, trees, and mountains. The wall drew so much attention that Fred wanted to keep me employed. He hired me to be a cashier with his foster brother Chris. Me and Chris became the best of friends from working side by side. We were stealing money out of the cash register to go buy weed. I got so tight with Chris and Fred that I wanted to be around them all the time. When I got paid I would give Pam my money and go home with Chris and Fred to spend the night. I started spending less and less time with Pam; and more time with Chris and Fred. I Noticed a beautiful Puerto Rican lady in Fred's yard waiting on his arrival.

Once we got out of the car, Fred walked over to the car and cursed her out by saying, "Bitch where have you been?" She replied, at the movies" He said, "bitch, you didn't ask me if you could go to the movies"! I walked over and interrupted their conversation saying "Fred is that any kind of way to talk to a fine lady??"! She replied "thank you.!" He told me to shut the fuck up and stay out of their conversation, and raised his foot up like he was going to kick me. I replied; you must think that I am one of those soft-ass niggas you hired to build that wall. Don't you raise your DAMN foot at me. After, that I noticed that girl kept checking me out. This was my first shot at getting revenge at him for telling me about the time he had been with Pam. After running the store, I saw more and more of the Puerto Rican lady and that's when I found out that her name was Maria. Maria was pecan tan, had dark, brown eyes, was about 4 feet eleven inches tall with beautiful Jet black hair hanging down her lower back. "Business was going good for Fred. As a matter of fact it was going so good he bought a night club." The name of the club was "Club Elite". Fred hired me and Chris as bartenders. As business got better I saw less and less of Fred and more of Maria. Fred had a lot of women, But Maria was his main woman. One day when Fred was with one of his other women out of town, Maria dropped by the club looking for him. She stepped to the bar and asked where was Fred? I responded by saying; "Baby you don't want to know where Fred is at. She said "yes I do and where is he?" I said you better take a drink first. I gave her the most expensive drink "Hennessy cognac." She took a drink and turned to me for an answer. I said Fred is with another woman in Winston Salem. She was shocked from the response. She told me to give her another drink. I filled the glass to the rim this time and she drank it straight without bringing the glass down from her mouth. She quickly asked me did i have any reefer or a joint to smoke. I told her that I didn't have any on me; but I got some at home. She asked me how far do you stay from the club. I said 3 blocks. She responded by saying, can you leave the club right now.? i said let me see if Chris can Cover for me. So I quickly shut the first bar down and ran to Chris' bar up stairs. I said Chris i need you to cover for me, because, I am trying to get some pussy tonight. He asked was i going to be gone all night. i told him that if I get this pussy that I ain't coming back. He said go ahead, just be here in the morning to help him run the store. I quickly walked back over to Maria to ask her was she ready to go. she said yes. Before leaving, I grabbed a bottle of cognac to take with us. I knew once I left this club with Maria, that I was going to get the pussy. My mind was working a mile a minute, thinking of a way to get my $20.00 bag from up under the mattress with Pam at home. I had Maria park the car and stay in it about a half a block from the house. After leaving Maria in the car I ran to the house full speed hoping Pam was not there. I stuck the key in the door. I walked to the bedroom to get my reefer but to my surprise, Pam was in the bathtub. I had to move quickly to avoid questions., Pam yelled from the bath tub "Peanut is that you."? I said yeah baby it's me, answering and getting my reefer at the same time. As I was moving quietly towards the door, Pam yelled "peanut come and wash my back." That's when I shut the door behind me. I ran full speed back to Maria's Car. After seeing me running she cranked up the car opened the door and let me in. While we were going down the road I started rolling hog leg joints to get this woman high as hell. After we smoked a half a joint we were parked in front of Maria's house and she asked if I wanted to come in her well furnished apartment. I accepted the invitation without a doubt. As we entered her house she quickly disappeared in the bathroom and took a shower. I continued to roll joints and pour her a drink. When Maria came out of the bathroom she was half naked, with two gold balls in her hands. She looked me directly in the eyes and said she didn't need Fred. Do you see these? I stared at the two gold balls in amazement wondering "What they were?" They were two solid gold balls the size of two marbles on a chain she used to masturbate with. As I got a good look at them I knew what they were. So I said, you don't need those balls tonight because I am here. Maria and I began to drink and smoke and drink and smoke Until we were high as a kite. Tha'ts when I began flirting with her and she made a pallet on the floor; and we had sex for 2.5 hours. After having sex with Maria we both fell asleep in each others arms. Early that morning she offered to take me home, but I felt damn good so I decided to walk the five miles. After walking 5 miles to the store I noticed Chris was asleep behind the store counter so I snuck up on him, stuck my finger to his nose and told him to smell this. He took a deep breath to inhale my fingers. I said "Do you smell that pussy? Do you smell that pussy?" I was so excited about me and Maria, I had to tell somebody and that somebody was Chris, because I could trust him. I knew that he was not going to tell rFred after all the money we stole out of the cash register, and all the bee we stole out of the cooler. Within 15 minutes of talking about the exciting night I had with Maria, I noticed her car pulling up in the store parking lot. She had brought me food from Hardees. She gracefully walked in the store, grabbed me from behind and said "hey baby I bought you some breakfast". I thought Maria was coming to the store to check on Fred but she was coming to bring me some breakfast. I felt like a damn king screwing Freds main girl. So in return, I went out to the car and filled it up with some of Freds free gas. Thank god Fred didn't see some of this because he would have a fit. After the store had closed, me and Chris were on our way to the club to go to work bartending. Fred was nowhere around. The only time Fred would show up was to pick up money at closing time from the store and club. He was spending most of his time with his new lady in /winston Salem. I was spending most of my time with his main woman, Maria. As the night went on I noticed Maria when she came through the door dressed to kill from head to toe. She came directly to the bar smiling and looking like a beautiful goddess. When she approached me, she said hello baby do you want to dance. This woman was looking so good I had to accept this invitation. I quickly came from behind the bar; we walked on the dance floor and started dancing nasty. Maria made me forget all about Pam, "I didn't give a damn about Pam and she didn't give a damn about Fred. "It was all about us!" as the music stopped playing we walked back towards the bar, I poured her a drink of her favorite beverage, Cognac". She leaned across the floor and whispered in my ear, "do you want to go home with me tonight?." I ran upstairs to the second bar and asked Chris could he cover for me again. He replied; you are going home with Maria again ain't you?. I said yea in a laughing manner. He gave me the okay to leave just as long as I was at the store to work in the morning. As I walked back towards the bar where Maria was standing, she stared at me from head to toe. So I pimped behind the bar and grabbed a fifth of cognac, threw the bottle over my right shoulder and put my left arm around her waist and pimped out of the club with her. As I walked her to the car like a gentleman, I opened her car door and let her in on the passenger side. As we were driving out of the parking lot, a Buick 225 followed us. I could feel Pam's presence all around me. But I continued to go on with Maria. We rode a quarter of a mile down the road when suddenly someone behind us kept hitting their bright lights. We continued to drive about two more blocks; the bright lights car flashed again. I was getting nervous so I told Maria to make a sharp right turn on the side road. She made a sharp right turn but the car with the bright lights followed. I told Maria to made a left turn, but the car proceeded to follow. The car was still an our tail. I knew it was Pam. I panicked and slid down in the seat and said ah hhhh, that's my girl Pam. Maria said don't Worry baby I will lose them. I could hear Maria's car accelerating. After lying down in the seat of the car for about 10 minutes scared as hell; Maria said "you can get up now I lost them". Within 2 Minutes We were in front of Maria's House.

No-one was in Sight! I felt relieved. As I got out of the CAR I Quickly Ran to Maria's Side of the Car, Opened the door like a gentleman Should, and planted a Wet Kiss on her lips. I reached in the Back Seat to Grab the Bottle of hennessy Cognac and Proceeded to Walk Maria into the House. Maria quickly took off her Clothes. I followed Suit. She was lying on the bed with her legs gapped Wide Open. I was ready to Pound her, When Suddenly, I heard to loud Knock at her front door.

"I was Pissed"! I told Maria "If that's Fred I'm going to tell him it's you & Me." She agreed! So I quickly Put on my Pants & Shoes to answer the front door. I tried to Peep out of the peep hole on the door, But someone had there Finger in front of the hole. Plus, they had unscrewed the front Porch light. I Continued to take the locks off the door from the inside to Open it. The door was half Open when a fist Struck me on top of my head, I reacted out of instinct to Swing BACK and I threw a Wicked Right hand. "It landed Solid" because whoever was Swinging at Me Stopped Swinging'!

I heard them hit the ground! My curiosity was getting the best of Me. So I Stepped outside to Screw the Porch light in. When I looked down to see who I hit "I Couldn't believe My eyes." It was Pam! She was Knocked out Cold from the devastating Blow to the jaw. I quickly Bent down to give her medical Attention. As I held her in my arms, She jerked out of My arms crying'& cursing' at Me. "You Rotten bastard . . .

I'm going to kill your No-good-Ass.! My Mind wondered how She had known I was there. Pam's girlfriend's driving the Buick 225 Knew Where Maria lived. So as maria drove the Car back towards her home, she took the Highway to Elude them, But Pam girl-friend took a Short-Cut to maria's house. They Were Parked Across the Street in Some bushes waiting on Our arrival. Pam quickly ran to the car to get a horse shoe stake. I Was trying to explain to Pam that i came over to look for Fred but she wouldn't listen. She came running towards me with the iron pipe in her hand to hit me in the head, so I threw my left hand up to block the blow when suddenly I felt a sharp pain run through my arm. Pam had snapped my wrist with the iron pipe so I chased her to her girl friends car. She jumped in the passenger side and locked the doors, I yelled at her through the window and said that I am going to kill you bitch. She replied that all your shit will be cut up when you get back to the house. I yelled to her don't touch my damn clothes. They continued to drive off when I went back into the house. When I approached Maria's bedroom she was still laying there with her legs gapped wide open ready to have sex. I had already been busted by Pam and I was not about to turn this Pussy down laying in front of me. As we proceeded to have sex I didn't last 2 minutes before she asked me "baby whats wrong?, is that it?I said what the hell do you mean is that it? I just got my arm broken by my girlfriend. Maria had remorse for me and offered to take me to the hospital. I told her just take me home. We drove toward Pam's apartment; I told Maria to let me out before you get to the apartment and I will walk from there. Me and Maria departed with a kiss. I continued to walk towards the apartment; as I got closer to the apartment, I noticed that all my clothes were cut up and lying in the yard. Anger fell upon me. As I entered the front door, no one was there to be heard so I cut the TV on and started crying from the pain in my left arm. Suddenly I heard women's voices coming from the back door. It was Pam and her three girl friends. When they entered the living room all 3 women started laughing at me. It pissed me off so bad I picked up a crystal ash tray and chased them out of the house. I ran back to the couch and started crying even more from the pain. Again I heard their voices enter the living room and they were still laughing. I started crying harder and picked up an ash tray and threw it at them. This time Pam entered the apartment by herself. She broke the silence by saying "what the hell were you doing with that bitch at her house?. I told her the same lie that I told her at the house; that I was looking for Fred. She had sympathy for me and tended to my wounds. Two days later my left arm wasn't getting any better so I asked Pam to take me to the hospital for x rays. My right arm had been snapped in two and the bone was growing crooked. The doctors had to rebreak my arm and mend my bones back together, and put a cast on it. After leaving the hospital I had Pam drop me off at Freds store. Chris was the only one there, so I told him about the incident, but I proceeded to work. Later that night when it was closing time, I caught a ride over Freds house with the bouncer of the night club. Fred's maid let me in; he was in the back laid up with one of his many women. He entered the kitchen and stared me in the eyes. This was revenge by me telling Fred how I screwed Maria and ate her pussy in his face. I broke silence by saying "guess what", "guess what?"He said what? you been pounding Maria?. I said damn how you know?. He said, I have my ways, now get the fuck out. I said what you mean get the fuck out?" He replied; just like I said, get the fuck out. I begged and pleaded with Fred that I didn't have a way home. Fred told me to get home the best way I can. As I began to walk down Fred's long drive way; I noticed Fred's carport light came on. When I looked back I saw Fred unleashing his six well trained doberman pinschers; My eyes got bigger than a bo-dollar so I hauled ass out of Freds yard running down the street. I left Fred's dogs about a quarter of mile running in fear. When I looked back there was not a dog in sight. I ran to one of his neighbors house's and caught a ride to Lexington; back to Pam's house and waited to go to work the next day. When I entered the store Chris said he had some bad news. He said, Peanut, Fred don't want you back in the store no more. He found out you were fucking his girl. The only thing I wanted was my three day pay; which was $78.00. I told Chris don't try to stop me from going in the cash register to get my money. Chris backed up as I went behind the cash register. I then hit the no sale button but to my surprise there wasn't but $40.00 in the cash register; I told Chris to tell Fred I got $40.00 out of his cash register and I am going up to the night club to get the rest. After walking the half block to the night club and entering the door, I noticed Fred's bouncer. Fred told him the same thing. Don't let me in his place. I told him I just left the store and got $40.00 out of the cash register so I am coming up here to get the rest of my pay which is $38.00, so don't stop me! No one even touched me 'as I proceeded to walk towards the cash register. I hit the no sale button, grabbed $38.00, no more no less, and walked out of the club. After my encounter with Fred, I never saw him again. As I look back on my encounter with Fred, he could have easily had me Killed for Messing with his woman. But the purpose of Messing with Maria in the first place, was to prove My point. Don't get me wrong! Fred hurt me bad, with his sarcastic Words of having Sex with A woman I was falling in love with. But I wanted to pay him BACK by Any Means necessary. Even if it meant death!

Almost 3 Years had Past! Pam & I were still together in the longest relationship I've ever held on too. I'd became Very popular in the City of Lexington By women, MEN, Drug dealers, and the Lexington Police Department.

One Night I Went to the Bow-Knots Liquor House to drink a Couple Beers with a Ole friend named Mike. As we entered the liquor House

I noticed the house was full with faggots & Punks. Mike And I were the only Straight guys in the Place. A very Muscular Homosexual Over-heard Me tell Mike . . . "damn"—Mike it ain't nothing but faggots in this place tonight lets get the fuck out of here". As Mike & I were Walking towards the door, The Homosexual Approached Me, tapped Me on My Shoulder and said . . . "Who are you calling a damn Faggot? If you see a faggot you Slap him", I was amazed at the Size of this Man faggot HE was about 6'7, 285 lbs. With a Black dress & High heels. Most of all he was black as night.

As I looked in the Eyes of the faggot. He was towering over me. I was Very skeptical of fighting this big bastard, But he invited Me to a Challenge. I'm not about to back down to anyone let alone a damn punk . . . a Homosexual. My Blood was at the Boiling point of laying' this Big Bitch Out, But he Kept his hand in his purse. At the time I was Holding a Millers BEER Bottle in my hand that I had just Ordered from the BAR. "Yo-Baby, 'I'm Sorry if I offended you in any kind of Way, Cause what you do is your business, so I'm Completely Sorry if I Offended anybody, will you forgive Me".

The faggot looked directly in my eyes when I extended My hand to shake for forgiveness. "Well, I forgive you this time, But don't let the Shit happen again"! The faggot didn't Even get a chance to Complete the Sentence. as soon as He Extended his right hand from the Purse he was

Wearing, I laid the Big Bastard Out With a miller's Beer Bottle. I Stood over him Saying' . . . In order to be the Best, you gotta beat the best baby! woooooooh as I walked off I heard My Buddy Mike telling Me to "run"! I looked over My Shoulders. I Saw 12 or 13 Homosexuals running towards Me, including the Big bastard I just laid out with the beer bottle. I Struck out running full Speed, They Chased me ¼ of a mile Down the Road, when Finally I Saw a 2 by 4 board lying in the middle of the Road. I managed to Bend Down, GRAB IT!, turn around and let them see the 2 by 4 Board. They were Bumping into each other trying' to put on the Emergency Brakes. Now the tables were turned, I was in Control. I Chased their Asses all the Way back towards the liquor House. They were Screaming like Women who just saw Godzilla or some damn Body. I was yelling" Ooh Hell, I'm gonna Split your fucking heads Wide Open Now! "Come back here". As I was Chasing them, I heard a Woman Voice Saying' . . . Ay, Ay, Ay, you don't need to be Chasing them, Stop baby, Come here!

As I Slowed Down to heed the woman's voice, I noticed those faggots Still running full Speed around the Corner, Yelling & Screaming thinking I'm Still Chasing them With the Big ass Stick. After they were Completely Out of Sight, I managed to stop and glance at the Nice looking lady who was Calling Me.

"Come here Baby", What's going on with you and those girls?, I replied in a Angry manner. them ain't "no damn girls, They have nuts bigger than Mine. She grabbed me by the right arm telling Me . . ." Baby, you don't need to be Chasing them. Please . . . let me Buy you a drink. (Those were the Magic Words.) My name is Tammy, what's yours? Peanut. Well, Peanut let's go over to this liquor house so can buy you a drink. I accepted Tammy's invitation. As we got to drinking a Couple of glasses of the Cheap Gin, I Started asking Tammy Questions . . . How old are you? 42! Where do you live? South mount! You got a Boy friend? No! I'm Single! Why? Because I'll take you to my Crib and Fuck the Shit out of you I Replied in a Bold Manner! "Boy, you can't handle this Pussy"! She said With Confidence. "there is only One Way to find Out" I said sarcastically, She spun around on her heels and Said "Come on"! Now I was facing a Challenge, I wanted to prove to this woman that I can back my Words Up! As we Started walking down the Street towards My apartment, Pam & My apartment. I had Everything timed Out. Pam was working 3rd Shift. It was 4:00 Am. I had exactly 3 hrs. to fuck Tammy and have her out of the house before

7:00 A.M. When Tammy and I reached the apartment It was 3:30 A.M, So I had only 2½hrs . . . to handle things. As we entered the apartment, Tammy noticed Pam's Picture on the Coffee table. She Said in a frightening manner! "Peanut, I know her. That's Pam! "She's crazy"! "girl, that's My Cousin, She don't live with Me! "Come and Show me what you're Working with". She Hesitated, But She gave in once She Saw me getting undressed. Within 3 minutes, we were in bed going at it like there was no tomorrow! We both were hollering like Wild Animals. Within an hour of having rough Sex, we both fell aSleep on top of One another. Before I Could react, I heard Pam Yelling & Screaming in the bedroom, "Peanut"! "What the fuck is this Shit?". Bitch, get your nasty Ass out My damn House. When I focused My Eyes, Pam was Kicking Tammy Ass all over the Bedroom. I Could barely react from the Cheap Gin I had drank at that damn Liquor House "STOP! Stop hitting that girl we didn't do nothing. But Pam was steady putting her foot up Tammy Ass, I Watched, But I could not react. After Pam ran Tammy out of her house, She came back for Me, "You nasty bastard", Get the fuck Out! "girl, we didn't do nothing, She just wanted a place to stay." As I observed Myself, I was Butt Ball naked, I Even had dry Sperm on my Stomach from having Sex with Tammy that Morning! "Motherfucka, you gon get the fuck out My house one way, or the other," But I Continued to Stick to My story. "We Didn't Do nothing!"

Suddenly, Pam disappeared out of the front Door. I fell back to Sleep, When I heard a loud Knock at the bedroom Door! Knock, Knock, Knock!!! "Who the Fuck is it"! Lexington Police, I was Still feeling Tipsy, "Come the Fuck in."! When I looked up from being under the covers, I noticed Pam & 3 officers in the Bedroom doorWay! that's him", I want him out of My damn House. I yelled back in Anger, "I 'm not going no damn where, I pay the Bills here, My name is on the Deed too", "you all get the Fuck out My damn House" After hearing me say that, the 3 officers left But Pam stayed behind to say, "You Rotten Bastard" "I'm going to get you out of My house"! Fuck You! Fuck You! Fuck You! I sarcastically expressed!

Within 20 minutes, the Police were back asking me questions about my name being on the Deed. I was lying My ass off, Pam never had My name on the Deed with her. She was doing everything! So the Officers took me up town for trespassing. The magistrate let me Sign my own Bond Stipulating that I don't go around Pam or her apartment.

I Walked from the Court house Building back towards Pam's apartment, I had to think of an excuse to get back with her, and get My Clothes from her house. Soon I was at the front Door and She was in the door way crying. I thought of the best lie I Could think of. I Stared Pam in her Eyes, begging' & Pleading her to forgive me. I Told her That I was sorry! I was only trying' to See Which Woman was the best women in Lexington. I gave her My Good Word that I would never make a foolish Mistake again. Well, Pam Accepted Me back into her house! But things weren't the same. Afterwards Pam was out for revenge! And She was aiming to Get it! She started going Out all different times of the night. Now the Shoe was on the other foot! One morning, Pam, & I had Sex! She fell aSleep afterwards, But I decided to Stay Up and draw her nude lying in bed. Well, the paper I was drawing Pam on had names of all the Woman I had Sex with Since I was Staying' in Lexington. As a matter of fact the paper had 14 female names on it, But I thought It was a Scrap piece of paper, So as soon as I finished drawing the nude Picture of Pam I woke her Up to Surprise her by giving it to her. She Stared at the nude Picture of her Sleeping. I noticed when She was looking at the drawing She was holding it up towards the light. She noticed Writing on the back of the paper. It said, "All the Woman I've had Sex with Since I've been in Lexington"! Plus the Women's names. Before I Could react to what She was reading, She quickly Jumped off the Bed and Ran into the bathroom! Again I found Myself trying' to Make Up another lie to Cover my Ass. "But to NO-avail"! Pam Stayed out All Night searching for the Women on the paper. I didn't realize What was going on Until I went Out looking for Pam at a Night-Club. When a friend asked me "what's Wrong With Pam?I Said "What the hell are you talking About"! he Said, Pam has cut 8 or 9 Women with a Straight Razor. I Was Shocked! Finally, I walked back to the apartment only to find Pam asleep in bed, She was tired & exhausted from Running the Streets. I eased My Way to her Purse. As I rambled through the Purse, I Saw the Paper I drew her picture on. I Unfold the Paper and turned to the drawing on the Other Side. I noticed 10 names we Scratched out. This told me that she had cut these Women up! Luckily not one of the women pressed Charges on her. So One night I began to Spy on her, She was in a Liquor house drinking and flirting With A Guy. That's when I went Slap off! I eased My Way into the Liquor House and demanded that She Come home, SHe was Scared shitless. She Knew from the look on my face that I was Ready to Flip.

I Asked her Once again . . . "Come on Pam, If you don't get your ass up from this table. I will turn this Son-of-a-bitch Out." All of a Sudden, I Snapped. I turned the table over that She was Sitting at. The Table flipped twice in mid air. I turned to her again and Said, "Get the Fuck up! She Started Crying in Fear. Someone Snatched me by my shoulder, it was the bouncer of the liquor house. I drew Back and threw a Wicked Right hand, Catching him Right between his Eyes. He fell Back Against the Kitchen Stove and fell forward, flat on his face, he was Knocked out Cold. Then I turned my Attention Back to Pam, demanding her to get the fuck up. I Could See from the Corner of my eye, the Guy She Was flirting with was Coming towards Me. But he knew Pam was My woman so He didn't intervene. I grabbed Pam by her hair and yanked her on her feet. But Someone Stole me on the Right Side of my Jaw, the lick grazed My Jaw. It was bouncer! He was back up on his feet again and I Pushed Pam in the Corner of the Kitchen So She was out of harms way. Now I turned my Attention Back to the bouncer! He had his guards up Ready to do battle, But I was too quick for him. I threw punch after punch after punch Until his Eyes Rolled back in his head. This time he fell face first on the wooden floor. If My punches didn't lay him out his fall To the floor did. As I turned to Pam, she was Still in tears. I Asked her for the last time to come on. After Seeing what I did to the Bouncer She managed to Work her way Outside. When She made it to the Edge of the Street. I turned Back to look over My Shoulders. Almost 45 People were in that Liquor House, But all Eyes were on me. So I broke the Silence Saying . . . "Does Anyone want To come and Rescue her?." To No-avail The crowd was Speechless when I Slapped Pam down the Road! She was crying; "Is somebody going to help me?" But no one came to her Rescue. When We Reached the apartment. We Both were in tears. I was in tears because I was going to lose her. Pam was scared of Me Now. She had never seen this Side of Me & neither Had I. I was going CRAZY, so I decided to depart from Pam and Move back to Salisbury. I figured it would be for the best; Either I Would wind up Killing her, or she Would End up Killing Me. During the 4 ½ Year love Affair with Pam, I Had 4 assaulting a female Charges, and 3 2nd degree trespassing Charges filed against Me. I Spent Over 2 Years in prisons & County jails over the love quarrels. Today Pam is happily married and having a lot more things in life than she Ever had. To this very day I have never seen Pam again! Why! Because the City of Lexington N.C. Recommended THAT I never Come back in their town ever again.

Rosa Parks endured many obstacles but never lost faith. (Her legacy lives on)

VOLUME 3

In 1989-90, I was AT THE BOTTOM ONCE AGAIN! Running the Streets of Salisbury & East Spencer, Strung out on CRACK-Cocaine. I found myself living in different CRACK houses, doing Any & Everything to Support My habit. It Seemed like the Whole town was smoking Rock. One day I went to My Aunt Jackies House to get me Something to Eat. I noticed she was sitting in the living-Room pissed off. I Asked her what was wrong?! She Said that young ladies had Stolen her Money. My Aunt told me She was in her Beauty Shop fixing hair when a lady named Toni Knocked on the back door to Set an appointment. But Toni had a crime partner named Tonya that was waiting at the front door of My Aunts house. While Toni was keeping my Aunt company in her Beauty Shop, Tonya snuck through the front door To Steal My Aunts Purse. After My Aunt told me what the two Rogues had done, I went out on a Rampage looking for them. growing up in my Aunts House wasn't Peaches & Cream. My Aunt Jacqueline Jackson Worked hard to Make ends meet while, raising Me & My older brothers," plus her own Son wasn't an easy task. With the Good Lords Help! She managed to raise all 3 of us. Memories Flashed back through time, to when she first took ME & My Older brother in her house. I was 5 yrs. Old, My older Brother was 7 when a cab dropped us off at her step. My Aunt was only 18 yrs. Old But she managed to raise us Until OUR teen-Age years. My Father died When I was Seven years old. I remember My Auntie Coming home from the hospital crying'. HER Brother which is My Father died of a heart attack at a young age of 28 years Old. My Aunt Did her very best to Keep My brother& Myself happy. I remember my Aunt trying' to Run a Liquor House, and Selling Reefer to keep food on the table for us.

But Now the only thing I Could think of was how hard She worked for her Money. She wanted us to become Somebody in life Besides a Nobody!

As I walked the streets of East SPENCER wondering Where The Two Dope heads were hanging' out at, "It hit me"! Broad street", had all the drug dealers" many of them were using the apartments (selling there). So I decided to hang out with them for a few hours. Within an hour and a ½ My patience paid off. I noticed the two Women who ripped My Aunt off for $178.00 dollars getting out of a CAR Walking towards one of the drug dealers I was Standing Beside. They both had a hand full of Money looking For the best bargain. little did they Know that Jacqueline Jackson was my Aunt. So I pretended to be Dumb-founded as if I didn't Know what was going on. I was waiting on the perfect opportunity to Make My Move. "Hello Jessie", do you have Something nice for fifty dollars. "Toni Said Excitingly"! Yeah baby I want to Cop a fifty piece of Rock also Tonya said as if she was the ring leader.

I Could See Jessie reaching in his pocket for the large Amount of Rocks he had in A plastic bag.

Jessie picked out 3 $20.00 Dollar Rocks to give to Toni, She gave him fifty dollars, and Waited on Tonya to Make her transaction. Tonya was Excited from Seeing Toni's Rocks, so She asked Jessie what will he do for Sixty Dollars. Jessie Reached in the plastic Bag to pull out 4 $20.00 Dollar Rocks and gave them to her. Now was the right time to Make My Move. As soon as they started walking fast toward the CAR. I walked behind them, and grabbed both women by their necks, yanking the Smallest of the two down to the ground. My Eyes were Shooting Sparks at both Women. I was Choking Tonya more than I was Choking Toni. After almost 30 Seconds of Choking both girls. I let Toni's neck go and turned to Tonya, I. drew my fist BACK and Caught her Right between the Eyes, She went tumbling over the Car. Then I drew my attention to Toni! HER Eyes were Shocked with Fear. I Start Slapping & Slapping' her Until My hand became numb, "I was Uncontrollable"! As The Drug Dealers watched with their mouths Open, they Couldn't believe what they were Seeing." They thought I was going CRAZY, But Not one of them knew that the two Women had just Ripped My Aunt off for $178.00," I jumped on the two Women Until there was no more Wind in Me." As I let the two bitches up, Jessie asked me why was I beating on them. I told him that they had Ripped My Aunt off for $178.00 dollars. I had both Women Sent personally back to My Aunts house for another Ass-Whipping.

When My Aunt saw them, She came out of the house with her 25 automatic pistol. My Aunt was planning on Busting Caps in both women's asses. As She approached Tonya With the BARREL pointed to her head, She felt the girl wasn't worth going to prison for. So She turned the pistol around only to hit the Girl in the head, But the GUN went off and Shot herself in the wrist," My Aunt was Bleeding heavily! "So My Uncle rushed her to the Hospital for Medical treatment and That was A turning point in My life! I Really Cared about My Aunt. Even today I'm overly protective over her! I Respect her very much because of what She's been through in life. And may the LORD Continue Blessing and Keeping her under his Wings!

After the incident I had with the two Dope head girls, Well-Known drug Dealers wanted to hire Me for their personal protection. Some even had helpers that Sold Rocks for them. I found Myself Watching Over inexperienced drug dealers to make Sure they wouldn't get Robbed through the late night hours of the Night. I became so Well-known, the drug dealers gave me a nick name . . . PEANUT, the "HIT MAN!" I Would Keep other drug Dealers from Selling drugs on their territory. They Even supplied Me with guns in case things got too hectic,. but,. In the late hours of the night I would end up Selling the guns for A Couple of CRACK Rocks. I went from One drug dealer to another Using My fighting' Skills.

Early in 1992, I was Working for this drug Dealer name Joe. He told me to Collect $300.00 Dollars from a Small time Drug dealer named Mike. I Saw Mike at the Store that Morning. I approached him about Joe's Money! I told him . . . "Mike, Joe Said for Me to Beat your ass if you don't pay him his Money." He Replied. "Motherfucka, Do what you Gotta Do!" He put his guard up to Defend himself. I was sizing the Boy up to Knock him Out! Before Knocking him out, I Asked him how old was he. HE Said, "I'm Seventeen Why?" I had made a Vow to Myself-never to jump on a Minor! So I quickly dropped My guards, and told him that he was to young for Me. I was 29, he was 17. I wasn't trying' to go to Jail for Beating up a Minor. Suddenly, Mike Jumped in his CAR and drove off. About 20 minutes later, I was Standing in front of a Convenience Store When I heard guys telling me to Run. Mike was Coming Around the Corner looking for me with A. .380 Hand gun. It was too late to React. Before I Got Myself turned Around, he was Right in My face. I noticed the Chrome Plated .380 in his left hand. He walked up on me and Stole Me directly in the jaw. THEN, he took two Steps back and Shot Me in my right thigh. "I Begged him for dear life not to Shoot me again.!" It Paid off! He got in his CAR and drove Off!

The Bullet went straight through My Upper thigh! the pain was unbearable, So I asked a drug dealer who witnessed Mike Shooting Me, for a Rock to ease the pain. He felt Sorry for Me.

He went into the Convenient Store and told the owner to Call me an ambulance. The owner quickly dialed 911 When the drug dealer came out of the Store. I begged him again for a Rock to ease the pain, he reached in his pocket and gave Me a Rock. I quickly took the Rock and put it on My pipe, held the pipe to my mouth and Smoked the Rock in the Store parking lot. I Could feel the drug easing away the pain. I began to follow the drug dealer who gave me the Rock, "He knew the police & ambulance were on the way. He went to some near by woods to hide, but I Stayed close to him. He told me to Stop following him because the police were on the way to the Store looking for me. Suddenly we heard a loud Siren from a distance away! They were almost a block away from the Store. The drug dealer panicked. "He Struck out running away from me. "I wanted to Run behind him, But I couldn't keep up from the gun Shot Wound. Suddenly, I Could See the police from the Wooded area, and they could see me Standing in the path way of the Woods looking dumbfounded. I heard the Officer yell . . . PEANUT! "Come here!" The officer Caught me by Surprise, I had no choice but to heed to his call. I quickly threw the CRACK-pipe beside a CAR tire that was in the Woods, and Walked towards the police Officer. I noticed a Crowd of people gathering. When I got Closer to the Officer, I noticed the ambulance, Fire Trucks, and Sheriff Cars in front of the Store. The officer Asked . . . PEANUT Have you been Shot?"! I Said, "Yeah, Why?" he Said, "Where at? "I Unbuttoned my Pants, pulled them down below my Knees To let the Officer Observe My Bullet Wound. I Could see a hole that held daylight Running from front to back. This was my first time Observing the gunshot also, I was in the Parking lot with My Pants Pulled down to my Knees Showing the Police officer Without a bother in the World. The paramedics came over to give me medical attention. They told me to lay down on the stretcher, But I refused to. I was feeling numb from the powerful blast of Cocaine Rock I had just Smoked. The Officer Begged Me to go to the hospital, But I Kept Making up an Excuse Saying . . . "I'll go on my own time"! The only, thing I Was thinking about is that CRACK-PIPE Under the tire in the woods that I hid. The Police Officer tried his best to get me in the ambulance But I Kept Saying to Myself . . . "Ain't no way in hell I'm leaving This place without getting me another hit on that Pipe in those Woods". Someone in the Crowd ran to My Uncle's house and told him about me getting shot, so he came to the Store looking for Me. When he Saw me, I was pacing around the Cars in the Parking lot, arguing with the Cops about getting in that damn ambulance. "I Ain't going no damn Where! "I'll Get to the hospital on my own!" I kept Saying to the officers!" When my Uncle "*BUTCH*" Saw me Cursing & Yelling at the Officers & paramedics, he embarrassed the Shit out of Me! My Uncle Butch Jackson is built like Hercules, and doesn't play Silly games. I Remember when my Aunt Jackie, brought me a pair of Boxing Gloves for X-MAS, I tried to Show My Skills off at the Age of 15. He accepted My Challenge in those Boxing Gloves. My Uncle hit me so hard, My eyes rolled in the back of My head. I never felt myself falling, nor did I Remember getting' up from the ground. But . . . WHAT I DO REMEMBER IS . . . "SLEEPING THAT WHOLE CHRISTMAS DAY!

Now my Uncle had Me by the Collar of my Shirt, telling Me . . . "Boy, If you don't lay your ass down on that DAMN STRETCHER, I'm going to Knock your ass down! Lay the fuck Down!"

The only thing I could think of is that Powerful Knock out Punch he gave me that Christmas Morning. So I gently let the paramedics treat me and rush Me to the Hospital.

Within 25 Minutes, I was treated & released from the Hospital. I quickly eluded the Police from asking questions about who Shot Me. I Caught a ride from the hospital. I was trying My best to get back down to the Store. So I could get a blast on the Pipe.

When I arrived at the Store, the parking lot was Crowded with Drug Dealers & Users. "Everyone had heard about my little incident (getting Shot in the thigh). When I touched down in the store parking lot, I Started pimping like I was the baddest Man in the World. I had just taken a .380 Bullet and, I'm Still living to talk about it, I Said to myself. "PEANUT, "are you okay?" Everyone Kept asking me as if they were Concerned! "Hell Yeah,

CAN'T NO DAMN BULLET KILL ME". I said sarcastically "Somebody give Me a DAMN Rock". When I Said that they Said, PEANUT "Where's your Pipe?" We are going to hook you Up! I quickly Hopped to the Woods, looking behind the Car Tire for my Crack-Pipe. I felt a Sigh of relief, When I Saw it Still there, I grabbed it, while running back towards the Dealers, "they put 6 Crack Rocks on My pipe at One time." I was so excited to See so many Rocks on my pipe at one time. I quickly Melted the Rocks on the Pipe, just in case they Changed their minds about giving me So many. I wanted this to last Me all day, but they insisted that I Smoke the Pipe in front of them. They wanted to see how I would react to the varieties of Rocks! "They told Me to hit the Pipe with all my might,." like a dummy! "I hit the pipe so hard, that the liquid ran from the pipe, into my mouth. A Powerful Rush went through my head. I Could barely focus with my eyes. My heart started racing like a fast moving Race Car. I felt like something was Crawling all over my body. "Wicked thoughts ran through my Mind, I Started Seeing things that weren't really there. I was hallucinating," Seeing Snakes everywhere! I wanted to Come down, But it was too late! I Started taking off my Clothes," Stripping down to my Boxers, in the PARKING LOT. Everyone was laughing. But I didn't care, because, I wasn't concerned about them, I was concerned about over-dosing!" The feeling of taking too Much drugs is a scary feeling, but by the grace of God, he let Me live to See another day!

After Coming down from the horrifying high. I was talked about throughout East. Spencer & Salisbury as "the laughing Stock" of the town, people picked at Me behind my back, "Calling me Snake-Man & the Stripper!!!

That was only the beginning, "In 1994 I was on the Corner of Broad street hustling drugs, When I was approached by a white Man who was Selling a 12 gauge Shotgun. He only wanted 3 CRACK Rocks for the Gun.

I wanted the Shotgun so bad, that i gave him an extra 2 Rocks along with the 3 Rocks to beat out the other Drug Dealers.

I was so Happy to have that 12 gauge Single Shot-Shotgun! I was approached by different Drug Dealers to buy the gun . . . but i wouldn't have sold that gun for all the Tea in China!

That Evening, I rode in a Car with a friend to the Waffle house. I got Something to Eat. We were Sitting in the Car, When a Well-Known drug Dealer approached us looking for Some Ladies who Borrowed his Car. He was angry . . . he Stated! "Peanut, have you Seen Lisa & Joyce driving My Car! "I Said, "No, Whats-Up!"

He Said, "I'm gone Kill them bitches When i See them, i was asleep and they took the Keys off the dresser, and took My damn Car, he said, "You wouldn't want to kill them With this, Would you?" Revealing the 12 gauge from the Car! His eyes grew large, He said, "PEANUT," Let me borrow the Gun until tomorrow, i'll give you 6 Rocks right now and in the morning you can get it back! I Told him i Want My Shit back, bright & early in the morning. "He agreed that he would give my gun back in the morning".

It was 2 Weeks before I Saw him again, He Dodged Me every time he saw Me, until One day i Saw him talking to another Drug Dealer," Both Dealers was sitting in there Cars when i approached him about my 12 gauge Shot gun. He had his Cousin driving his CAR. The Drug Dealers name was 4 fifth and the young Drivers name was Lee. I walked directly to 4 fifth asking him about My Gun. He Said, that Lee had it. I approached Lee, he said that he would get it later on.

I tried to push the drivers Seat to get in the Car, but he wouldn't let Me, He Said that he would come back With the Gun. I felt like he was trying' to run game on me since he was not letting me ride with them, So i quickly Snatched his gold necklace from his neck, and told him when he come back with My Gun, I'll give him his necklace back. "He was pissed"! He threw the hand brake up in the Car and jumped out to fight Me. "This young Buck was no Match for me. He Charged me in anger," Swinging at Me!" I Ducked and Scooped him off his feet," "Slamming him into the Street, face first! Lee Rolled over on his back. I grabbed him by his legs," I told him, that "I Don't want to fight!" I just want my damn Gun back," After getting My point across, I let Lee up! He ran to the Car embarrassed and drove off! I still had his Gold necklace in my hand waiting on him to return. The local Dealers begged Me to Sell them the Gold necklace, but, I Refused them all, I was waiting for Lee's return with my 12 gauge. After waiting almost 10 minutes, I noticed Lee driving 4 5ths BMW Coming down the Road Speeding. I held up my hand letting him Know I had his necklace. I Saw a gun Barrel hanging out the drivers Window. A loud blast Went off! Buck-Shots hit Me in my pants, But not in My Skin, I picked up the up the Bicycle got on it, and rode quickly towards the bushes. I heard the Car tires Squeal from hitting on brakes. Lee was Angry, he wanted revenge. He wanted to Kill Me with My own Gun! I rode the Bike quickly through a nearby Pass on the other side of the Path. You could See more Drug dealers. I Spotted a Drug dealer name Tony, I yelled to him . . . "Tony, come here! I need to See you!" He came in the path asking me what was wrong. I Told him that Lee had just Shot at Me. I Explained to him what Happened. He noticed the beautiful Gold necklace I was holding in my hand. I offered to Sell the necklace to him for 15 Rocks and demanded that he buy me a motel to hide from Lee.

He told me to wait in the path until he got his Van. Within 2 Minutes, he was blowing the Car horn, letting me Know that he was ready. I quickly ran to the Van Scared to Death! Once I got in the van I felt Safe. Tony gave me 15 Rocks for the necklace and drove Me to a Motel up-town. Once I was in the Room I began to relax. I took a nice Hot-Bath, and afterwards, I ordered me Something to eat! Once I put Some food on my Stomach, I Started Smoking" Rocks after Rocks." I Smoked about 4 or 5 Rocks to build up my nerves. Suddenly, I was Calm. I wanted to go back to East. Spencer, and make Some Money, off the Rocks I traded for the Gold necklace. So I left the Motel Walking towards East. Spencer. When I reached East. Spencer City Limits. A friend Ran up to Me warning Me to go back where I Came from. I asked him Why?" He Said, that Lee & 4 5th had Shot up a Crack house looking for me, That they thought I was hiding out in the Place. I said to My friend . . . Whatever happens, Will happen! He looked at Me like I was CRAZY! I Continued to walk into East. Spencer waiting on My death to arrive. I Didn't Know what Kind of Car Lee & 4 5ths was driving. I just Continued walking the quiet Streets. After 5 or 6 hours of Walking the Streets in the late night hours,

Dawn was Approaching . I was down to my last 3 CRACK Rocks. I Didn't make Any money, Cause I was busy trying to Stay on guard after Smoking CRACK. It always Kept me alert of my Surroundings, Especially from the Police. I Would listen for footsteps creeping in the Bushes, looking for Cameras in abandoned buildings. I Would look at Dogs and See what they would be Staring at, or Why were they Barking. I Even Studied the trees to See if the Police were hiding in them in their Camouflage Clothing.

I had an eye for trouble!!!! And Something was telling me trouble was near. early that Morning I Kept Smelling Blood & Gun Powder. I Kept Saying to Myself. "I SMELL DEATH!" "I SMELL DEATH!" Suddenly, I Saw one of My Best Customers Riding the Streets looking for a buy, he saw me in his REAR-view mirror and I noticed he Put on his Right turn Signal to get around the block. I Quickly Ran through the back path way to cut him off. When I Reached the End of the Path. I notice 4 5ths & LEE in a parked Car Sitting 20 yards away from Me. "I was shocked" Both Guys were staring me directly in the eyes. I had to Make up an excuse quick about Lee's Gold Chain.

"Lee, I Got your Chain Fixed" I said with Terror in my Voice. HE Replied, "Where is it?" It's over Big Ed's house", "I Said, nervously"! So you think you can just Snatch some shit off My neck, huh! as he begun to get out of the Car I noticed a 44 Magnum in his right hand. I Started backing back in fear, he aimed it directly at Me. I wanted to run, but there was no where to run. Suddenly, I heard a loud Blast! The Bullet Struck me in the Abdomen, Cutting me a backwards flip . . . a Backwards Flip in the air. When I landed on the Cement, My Left leg was hanging on the back of my neck. My Voice Faded, The pain was unbearable. I Could See him walking towards me With the 44. Magnum reloaded. He stood over me saying . . . The next time you snatch a chain off my neck. I will kill your Black ASS! "I was Speechless" My lips Moved, But nothing Came out. I could see Lee walking back towards the Car and drove off. "My Life was flashing before my eyes". I could See people gathering around me, scared to touch Me from the CRAZY looking position the Gun Blast left me in. I heard a Distant Voice telling me to hang on, A Chopper is on the Way! "The Voice faded". I was going on an Unknown Journey in Space. My eyes Opened. I Could See the heavens & Clouds ABOVE. But it was from the Chopper flight taking Me to Winston-Salem Baptist Hospital.

I was unconscious for 2 days before Opening my eyes. I stared down at my legs, happy to See both legs was Still attached. I wiggled my right foot and Smiled I Wiggled my left foot, but, No Movement! So I tried it again. "still, no movement"! I Started Screaming for help, the nurse came running to my Aid. I was Crying' in fear, Asking her why I can't Move My legs. She Explained, I had just had Surgery on my leg. She said, the Gun Shot blew my Fibula out of Socket. I had an artificial hip replacement. And that I would have to learn to walk all over again. I Couldn't believe what I was hearing. I said to myself, It's a dream! Pinch Yourself PEANUT! Well, after realizing it wasn't a dream, i was determine to Walk again. They gave me physical Therapy for 2 days. The improvement was so great. They Released me from the hospital to go home. Soon My Aunt, Jackie was there to pick me up. She Encouraged me to Stay with her Until I was able to walk again. She was so Sweet to Me! She even gave me her own bed down-Stairs to keep Me from Climbing the Stairs to my Old room I once Stayed in, before I had Moved out. You See, I had in mind not to ever Move back home with My aunt. "When i reached the age of 18, I made a vow to never live there again." Why?because, my brother & I took the best Years of her life. Her teen-age years! She never really had a Chance to enjoy life for raising her brothers Kids, even today, I still hold that Vow! I found myself walking Up & Down the Street on Crutches trying to get used to walking on one leg. Suddenly I was in distance of a CRACK-house "a block away from my Aunt's house."

I managed to hop to the door, when I was greeted by some Drug users inside, they invited me in to Smoke a few Rocks with them. the local Drug Dealers would come over and Sell there Rocks in the house. I felt like that was my home! the only thing I had to do is wait on more dealers to come over and I would Stay high all night long. That same night 2 Drug Dealers Stayed over night to Catch sells Coming in the house. When I saw them falling to Sleep at the Kitchen Table i waited patiently for them to go into a deep sleep, they had been smoking blunts of Reefer the whole night. Within an hour, everyone in the house was Sleep! I wanted to Creep to the Table beside the Drug and Dealers and take the Money & Rocks out of their pockets. But I had to get my Crutches to get myself up from the low sitting Chair I was in. I Managed to reach the Crutches from the wall, and Hop to the Empty Chair beside the 2 dealers. I slowly eased my right hand in one of the drug dealer pocket and pulled out a Small Bank Roll of Money. But I wasn't Satisfied. I wanted the Rocks too. So I went back in for a Second Chance. It Paid off! I took the Bag of Rocks from his pocket. I was so excited, I didn't bother to Check the Other Drug Dealer. I needed to get out of there before someone Knocked on the door and woke Everybody up in the House. So I quietly eased away from the table with the Crutches Underneath My arms. And quietly Opened the door and walked Out unnoticed. As I Managed to make it to the Street, I ran into my Aunt, she had just left her house and was on her way to town to pay Some Bills.

She Asked Me from the Car . . . "Boy, "Why come you didn't come Home last-night!" You had me worried about you!". She Said with Concern. I told her that I was Okay! I quickly asked her for a ride Up the Road, She told me to get in . . .

That was a Sigh of relief. Now I was putting distance between Me and the Crack-house, the drug dealers were Sleeping at. I was 7 or 8 blocks away from the drug dealers when My Aunt dropped Me off. Now I was into Another Crack-house Smoking & Spending their loot. This is nothing proud to talk about. It just goes to show you how devious & Sneaky the drugs will Make a person. I was the best in stealing Other people's drugs. I waited patiently for them to go to Sleep in CRACK houses. Sometimes If I Couldn't get to the drugs in there pockets. I would take a Razor blade and Cut through their pants to get their Package of Rocks.

Today this is my Rock (Jesus Christ) "MY STRONG ROCK"

I Want you Readers to Know that the LORD has been good to me through the Years. I'm 37 years old! I've been shot 11 times on different Occasions., I've been Snake bit twice., I've had a heart-attack once, Stabbed twice, and overdosed on drugs, not to Mention an After Death Experience, in which, I choose not to talk about on paper. I Want to let the Readers Know that I'm doing Prison time. I was sentenced in 1998 for Robbery with a dangerous Weapon & Assault and inflicting Serious Injuries. I was Sentenced to 119 to 146 Months in Prison. My Release date is 2008. Certainly, I'm proud to Say that The LORD Spared my life for a very good reason. Today I'm Drug-Free. I've Accomplished a lot since I've Been in Prison and I've found Peace with the LORD.

I'm Striving to be a True Soldier in Christ. I've been in the Prison System 3 Years, I'm very proud to Say that I haven't touched Cocaine within the 3 Years I've been in the System, and It's not because I'm locked up! Almost any type of drugs you can name are flowing through the Prison Systems. Yes I'm very Capable of using Crack Cocaine, But I Choose not too! Crack-Cocaine Almost destroyed My life; Including the Relationship with my family Members. I've been in & Out of Prison over a Dozen times. Mainly Dealing with Drugs! This Book is a True Story Based on the Life of Charles Calvin Barber (A.K.A. "PEANUT)". I'm very proud to Say I still have my Auntie—(Ms. Jacqueline Alonia Jackson) Hanging by My Side! She encouraged me to write this Book to the World, So this is my testimony! PLEASE TAKE HEED to My Real life Experiences of what CRACK-Cocaine will lead too: *Prison* or *Death!* For those out there in the World, or in Prison, Using Crack Cocaine. I Encourage you to make that Change in your life Before it's to late, Because you may not be as fortunate as I. Take Time out to see what life has to Offer you, I've found my Destiny in life . . . and that is to be fair as I can be in life. OF Course with My LORD & Saviors help, because without prayers to My Heavenly Father, none of this would be possible. MAY God Bless!!!

www.ingramcontent.com/pod-product-compliance
Lightning Source LLC
Chambersburg PA
CBHW020345290526
45785CB00005B/2165